Wagner's excellent advice to school innovators is to keep it simple. He follows his own advice to great effect in this lively volume, focusing on key aspects of school transformation: clear vision, purposeful use of space, personalization, curriculum integration, community-building, and connection with the physical and temporal world beyond school. At every turn, he fills this framework with practical wisdom and concrete strategies, born of his experience teaching and leading in schools on both sides of the Pacific, for addressing the challenges of contemporary education.

- Rob Riordan, Co-founder of High Tech High and President Emeritus, High Tech Graduate School of Education

This is a must read for all innovative teachers and administrators wanting to shake up their schools with great teaching and learning! The Power of Simple is equal parts great pedagogy mixed with detailed strategies for forward thinking 21st Century schools. The book profiles Kyle's journey toward seeing his dream of an individualized, project based, passion and experienced driven program take shape through the Futures Academy at the International School of Beijing. Some of my greatest take aways from the book are Kyle's unique use of personalized scheduling, student centered learning spaces, and amazing integrated projects!

- Evelyn McCullough, Innovations Coach at Park Maitland School

This is not just a "must read", but it is a "must implement". The writing, as the title suggest, keeps the idea of innovation in education simple without overgeneralization. As I read The Power Of Simple, I kept my palm pressed against my forehead and found myself shouting, "duh" or "of course!". I am starting a project-based learning school in India starting a project-based middle school, and this book is invaluable. I have applied The Power Of Simple to my own practice, and I am seeing the benefits of Wagner's philosophy, The Power Of Simple, everyday. Beside the examples provided in the book, Wagner is very honest about the difficulties of enacting change, and this is crucial for all educators to understand: while keeping structures simple, one must build a positive school culture between adults and students, and keeping structures simple is at the start of it all.

- Anthony Conwright, Dean of School High Tech High Media Arts

In this book, you get a real sense of how a transformative education can look, especially at the middle level. The book is full of examples, optimism, and encouragement. It is good for those who already have started formulating their own vision for transformative education and would like some inspiration and ideas.

- Zachary Post, Head of Middle School at American School of Hong Kong

This book makes transforming schools into an achievable process. Other books on the topic are messy and unclear. Wagner breaks it down into simple tasks/modifications that educators can make immediately. As an administrator of a small international high school program, after reading this book, I feel I have to tools necessary to lead my faculty and students into the future of education. From scheduling, planning physical space, integrating curriculum, individualizing learning, to supporting teachers, I now have learned what is necessary for us to make education what it needs to be, for this next generation. Thank you Kyle Wagner for empowering me to make change immediately, and giving me the knowledge and confidence to transform my school.

Kate Hummel, Dean of Students Chongqing, China

The power of
SIMPLE

Transform your school by conquering the
standards, individualizing learning,
and creating a community of innovators

Printed in the United States of America
First Printing, March 2016
ISBN 978-1532769016
Create Space Publishing
San Bernardino, CA

DEDICATION

This book is dedicated to the greatest teachers I have ever known - my mom and dad.

ACKNOWLEDGEMENTS

This book would not have been possible had it not been for the giants who stood beside me. It is a culmination of their guidance, support, and patience that helped me become a better educator.

I would first and foremost like to thank my wonderful husband Roy, who forgave my absence as I belabored over this book, and encouraged me to speak up when I felt as if I had nothing valuable to say.

Thanks to my writing coach and friend Azul Terronez, who helped me simplify my message, insisting that only through honesty and humility could I inspire educators to action.

I would like to thank my best friend and brilliant graphic designer Nathan Mohle who helped with the branding for my business and book.

Thanks to my brother Chad Wagner, who served as an editor and coach in making my prose more readable and personal for readers.

Finally, and most importantly, I would like to thank the educators that have dedicated their lives to the betterment of others. You are my greatest inspiration.

TABLE OF CONTENTS

I quit my job, sold my car, terminated my housing lease and finished packing my bicycle into a small carrying crate. It was the last item of value I had left to my name. Its destination- Shenzhen, China. Whether or not it would make it there was completely left to chance. What was I doing? I was leaving behind my family, friends and most notably a job at one of the most innovative schools in the country, if not the world, for a place that had only recently allowed foreigners to teach in its international schools. A communist country so tightly controlled that I would have to use a VPN just to check my Facebook News Feed. I was leaving the land of the free to find my American Dream 3,000 miles away— in China. People thought I was crazy. Perhaps I was.

Sometimes it takes a crazy decision to actually find your sanity. I was sick of being stuck. On the outside, you would never know it. I hid it well. To others, I appeared the consummate idealist. Always smiling, focused on the positive, committed to new ideas, cheerful, optimistic and ever-changing; but on the inside, I was terrified of actually making a change.

Every time I considered making a change, the self- critic crept in. Why change? Kyle, it begged, don't forget that you teach at High Tech High — a school that has 2,000 students begging to get in. Where else in the world will you have the freedom to innovate that you have here? You get to help students create work of value that serves a purpose in the real world! The voice in my head served as a constant reminder to stay put, and not jeopardize everything I worked so hard to achieve.

And so I remained in that space for over two years. How I suddenly built up the courage to finally make the change will forever remain a mystery. It was neither an epiphany nor a near death experience that prompted a radical change. It was a self- realization that I was **born to create change.**

Fast forward to today. Because of that decision to leave everything three years ago, I landed the job of my dreams at an innovative international school in one of the most closed countries in the world. I was hired to create an adaptive "future school" within a school and make some radical changes in education. You see, it's not circumstance that holds us back. It's only ourselves.

Futures Academy at the International School of Beijing is a school without limits. Our schedules change every week depending on the learning experience. Our students present professional work each month to experts in the field. Visitors from around the world come to learn from us several times a year. It is an innovative, fully integrated program built around students exploring their passions and creating work of value in the real world. It's a school from the future built inside a school of today. Most importantly, it is a school that I could never have envisioned had I not first left my current position.

What if you were given the time and freedom to make major changes in school? Where would you start? What would the school look like? What would students learn? What opportunities would their schedules include? What would instructors teach? What would the classroom look like? Would you even need a classroom?

Helping you find these answers is what this book is all about.

Perhaps you find yourself in the same position I was in before risking everything. Who am I to create something so great? Deep down you yearn to promote and foster radical change in education but are too bogged down by the systems that currently exist. You know that you want to create a community of innovators and future problem solvers, but feel powerless with the lack of time and curriculum you've been provided. Perhaps your school has already granted you license to make major changes, but you feel paralyzed by the enormity of what that implies, not knowing how to take practical first steps.

This book will help make those first steps more simple and painless, providing you with the structures to bring about the greatest change and move forward. It is written by someone who used to be in the same position you are in now.

Real change is scary; which is why schools have avoided it for half a century. It takes vision, dedication, persistence and a commitment to our ideals. But it doesn't have to be as hard as we've made it. By helping you adapt and re-think some of the underlying structures of scheduling, planning, curriculum and assessment, you will feel energized to inspire the kind of learning you envisioned when you first became an educator.

This book is not about asking you to create another school that mimics *Futures Academy*; but rather, it is about inspiring you to create your own. It's about taking a few of the strategies you find most useful and adapting them to best fit **your** own needs.

Welcome to the power of simple.

CHAPTER ONE

KEEP IT SIMPLE

"Every journey begins with a single step." -Laozi

Do a few things and do them well

To create change in your school, you are going to need a crystal clear vision. Many educational institutions fail because they try to be too many things to too many people. It's impossible to blame them. Schools have the hardest job in the world, with the most stringent demands. If tightening things up and focusing on delivering rigorous standards, society complains that they are not allowing room for creativity. If allowing students to take multiple approaches to learning, people gripe that not enough focus is being placed on the curriculum. Therefore, for fifty- years schools have compartmentalized learning to deliver on every societal demand in isolation. But by trying to do everything, what in fact many schools have done, is actually very little.

The world is saturated with schools. If you typed in "local schools" in a Google Search box, regardless of the city, state, or province you live in, I am certain you would receive well over a hundred hits. Many will have pedagogies that are watered down with taglines that do little to define what they actually do. Something to the effect of "Empowering all students." "Teaching Students to be Successful." The waters become even murkier when scrolling down to the school's mission statement. Here is the mission statement from the infamous Dalton School:

The Dalton School is committed to providing an education of excellence that meets each student's interests, abilities and needs within a common curricular framework and reflects and promotes an understanding of, and appreciation for, diversity in our community as an integral part of school life. Dalton challenges each student to develop intellectual independence, creativity and curiosity and a sense of responsibility toward others both within the School and in the community at large. (1)

How has this mission statement specifically defined what the Dalton School actually does? The Dalton School promotes "an education of excellence that meets each student's interests within a common curricular framework." Do these two statements not sound contradictory? It's a system that desires to individualize learning for students through common structures. Wouldn't individualizing learning necessitate the creation of several distinct curricular structures? What does the statement even mean? In my humble opinion, I believe that this mission statement has created more confusion for its intended audience.

As school leaders, we need to model ourselves after successful businesses. The most successful businesses can create a clear and simple statement of who they are and a vision of what they want to become. Take Google for example. Here is a company that has, and will continue to revolutionize the way in which the world receives its information because it knows how to define what it does.

Google's Mission Statement: "Organize the world's information and make it universally accessible and useful." (2)

That's a pretty clear mission. Think of how easy it is to move a system forward with that kind of mission statement. Any new technology or decisions made within the organization can be evaluated by analyzing whether or not they help "organize the world's information and make it universally accessible and useful."

How do we create this clear vision as leaders in our schools? Answering this question involves finding a few key design principles to institute, and implementing them really well.

What's your sticking point as an educator? What defines your pedagogy? Finding and communicating those key ideas is what this section is about.

To individualize learning and create a community of innovators, you are going to have to be able to define what you do in a sentence or less. If you want to become even more definitive, you should be able to define what you do in only a few words. This will help simplify what you are trying to accomplish and ensure you are spending time doing the things you most care about.

Some schools are designed as *dual immersion models, creating global citizens through the immersion in foreign language.* Others are *arts based models, integrating learning around performing, visual and fine arts.* These mission statements are far more concise and concrete and allow for the creation of clear structures to help fulfill them.

ISB Futures Academy had to learn the profound lesson of simplicity the hard way. After two years of strategic planning, the ISB school board in cooperation with our Communications Department, Head of School, Deputy Head of School and various committees came up with five key strategic initiatives they hoped the *Academy* would achieve. These were the five initiatives:

- Increase relevant learning through authentic, compelling local and global engagements

- Optimize each student's capacity to learn through individualized experiences and opportunities

- Nurture the whole child, including social- emotional, academic and physical well- being

- Invigorate ISB's practice based on best research on teaching and learning methods and the changing realities of the 21st century

- Increase access to expertise and new learning through additional collaborative efforts and networks beyond ISB

There were well over hundred pages in the final document with matrices, graphs, activities, outcomes and complicated visuals to show how strategically ISB would achieve each goal. To the outsider, the document appeared flawless; a demonstration of the narrative mastery of brilliant adults. To the intended audience-children and parents in this case, it was yet another complicated structure to delay taking practical first steps.

Like our predecessors before us, *Futures Academy* facilitators vowed to be all things to all people; and we suffered because of it. We promised parents a new reporting system that captured cumulative data on students, reported on their progress, communicated results, and allowed project planning all at the same time. We promised we would focus all learning around student passion. We promised we would not use grades to evaluate students, but comment based benchmarks. In essence, we promised parents we would deliver on all the strategic initiatives and fix all the problems with the educational system in less than a year. We had done two years of planning before students even entered the room.

Not even John Dewey could deliver on such unrealistic claims.

And so in its first year of development, Futures Academy struggled. It was immersed in an identity crisis that could have been avoided if it had a clear vision it followed. And while we offered several innovative systems and opportunities for students, there were few of them that we did exceedingly well.

In year two, we are far wiser. We have narrowed our focus. Instead of promising everything that was first outlined in the school's strategic plan, we have promised only the following:

"ISB Futures Academy is an **innovative** learning **community** that empowers ISB and its students for a **changing global** society."

This mission statement has created a clear foundation as we explore new structures to improve student learning. More importantly, it has allowed us to create key design principles to help drive what we are trying to achieve. These design principles are what the rest of this book will be based on. They are outlined below:

⊘ **Flexible Scheduling and Space**: Futures Academy will design schedules and space in a way that is most relevant to the learning

⊘ **Integrated Learning:** Futures Academy will integrate learning around a common theme

⊘ **Individualized Opportunities:** Futures Academy will create individualized opportunities to help students explore their passions

⊘ **Relationships:** Futures Academy will create opportunities that allow students and facilitators to develop positive relationships

Ø **Real World:** Futures Academy will connect students to the world outside of school

What do you do well? What is your tagline? Instead of filling your classroom, school, or office with posters that demonstrate the several things you are attempting to do, narrow them down to a few categories that you can and will do well. This will help ensure you are expending energy on the things you care most about.

What does all this have to do with creating change, or transforming your school? How is it relevant? It's relevant because simplicity has a profound impact on the effectiveness of the overall system.

So, if you want to create lasting change in your school, help the system keep things simple and intimate.

The Power of small models

Simplifying the way we do things becomes exponentially easier when decreasing the size of our systems. In large systems, there are way too many structures to eradicate if hoping to make major transformations that will impact all students. Years of the status quo have come with layer upon layer of dysfunctional bureaucracies and managerial structures. Therefore, to ensure you have an influence on the overall system and institute long-lasting change, you must start by choosing the simplest route.

I liken it to political change. If you dialed up the white house, you would most certainly be directed to an automated system that gave you several options, none of which would put you in touch with the individual atop the system. Similarly, if you were to call up your district office or the federal minister of education, it would most likely be weeks if not months until you could engage in a personal conversation.

You must start from where you are. What changes can you implement at the grass roots level? What decisions do you have control over? Equipped with the clear vision you were able to create in the first section; you will be in the perfect position to implement far-reaching changes in all corners of the school. Perhaps you are a teacher with your own classroom to manage. Perhaps you are a middle school principal with teachers, office staff, and scheduling to manage. Perhaps you are a curriculum director with curriculum and standards to oversee. We are going to approach our work from a different angle. Rather than face the mountain of obstacles we must overcome to implement systemic change, we are going to start with the areas within our control.

Don't worry about the minutia of curriculum, scheduling, grouping, school culture, and practical strategies right now, those will become clearer later, for now, we are going to start with the change that has the most lasting effect: Empowering others. Let's make sure that as a manager, you first have broken up your oversight into smaller self- sustaining systems.

If you are a teacher, this means breaking up classrooms into small, interdependent groups. Maneuver the chairs in a way that fosters this kind of collaboration. Empower students by providing them specific tasks and then fishbowl strategies that demonstrate how to fulfill them. If you are an administrator and oversee a group of teachers, divide them into small integrated teams that have decision-making power. Work with them to brainstorm a list of tasks together that must be fulfilled in moving forward, and then delegate small committees to investigate and report out their findings. If you oversee a large school with several departments, find some shared common agreements, and then allow your departments to manage themselves.

When I was given the same blank piece of paper you now have in front of you, I immediately sought out systems that I knew to be successful. I researched educational models, business models, non-profit models and other managerial structures. What I found was that smaller systems are by default far easier to manage. Sure, there were a few of those large corporations that managed to move forward with a shared ideology, but those were few and far between. And naturally, they had far more to lose. If a small system fails, there are other parts of the organization to pick up the slack. If a large system fails, the organization goes with it. Therefore, if you want to implement change, start on a small scale. You will be able to implement far more of the changes that lead to greater systematic change. The future will rely on these small and agile systems, able to shift course if curricular goals or instruction becomes obsolete.

Futures Academy based itself on this premise. It was the pioneering ship that left port before the larger school steam liners had constructed their hulls. This massive institution's strategic plan would not have to wait five years to implement, but could be enacted right away.

So how did this school keep things small even as the system grew? They gave control of the system over to small interdependent teams. Our school within a school consists of a total of 7 facilitators spread across two grade levels. As such, we have the power to determine what students will learn, how they will learn it, and when they would be offered each experience. By handing over the decision- making power to a small team, the large school empowered us to make far more changes than it could make had it dictated them from atop the system.

Implementing change is still not going to be easy. What you must be willing to face is the fact that inevitably, you are going to experience some short- term pain. If you are a teacher seeking to divide your classroom into small interdependent teams, it's going to involve a lot of frustration, dysfunction, and headaches in the short term. And that has nothing to do with the fact that small systems don't work, it's just that your constituents have never been given this kind of responsibility and power in the past. Similarly, if teachers have been equipped with more decision-making power than they have had in the past, it's going to require constant support and outside facilitation to make sure they do not revert into a traditional way of doing things.

Again, creating real change involves empowering and entrusting your constituents to act on their own. This is not an easy task, and it's something that *Futures Academy* facilitators had to learn the hard way. About two months into the school year in *Futures Academy*, my facilitator team felt frustrated, overworked, stressed and unable to complete the monumental tasks placed before us. We had far-reaching ambition and way too much on our plates. Initially, we hoped that by delegating some of the tasks amongst ourselves, we would alleviate some of the stress. One facilitator was placed in charge of mentoring meetings, project development and documenting progress through photos and writing; one in charge of enacting and modifying schedules according to teacher needs; and one in charge of classroom display and projecting a positive image to the rest of the school regarding the progress of the program. Naturally, this alleviated some stress, but it did not have the long- term results we desired. We still felt powerless.

And that's when the epiphany came; we did not involve those we intended to impact in the change process.

We learned. Currently, we have several student "committees" in charge of the tasks vital to the success of the program. We have moved those we intended to manage into a position of authority, giving them the capacity to make decisions that work towards the betterment of the system.

Every one of you who reads this book has the same capacity to empower small teams to help transform your school. Here are a few tips to ensure they are successful.

- Create clear structures and time for the committees to meet.

- Lead initial sessions and pose the questions that will move the committees forward.

- Don't micro-manage. Entrust the process and reflect if the work is not getting done.

- Create spaces for small teams to share their learning with the broader community. If the larger team you intend to manage sees others empowered, they will develop their own self- efficacy to institute change.

- Cross-pollinate committees to give your constituents the opportunity to work with other members of the organization. A common sense way of doing this is by having committees set short- term goals and then re-assessing every six weeks.

In Closing

If you have made it this far, you have already completed the hardest work in school transformation! You have created a clear vision for the changes you want to make, established some key design principles and envisioned how to create the kind of small structures to deliver upon these principles. Well done. As you read these next sections, take your new vision statement and put it somewhere visible. This will allow you to process the plethora of strategies I will offer through the filter of your own vision. Remember to always keep the big picture in mind! Ready? Ok, now it's time to leave the forest and get into the trees.

CHAPTER TWO

FLEXIBLE SCHEDULING AND SPACE

"The measure of intelligence is the ability to change"
- Albert Einstein

Flexible Scheduling

How many of you remember your first day of middle school? I remember mine well. I pulled up to school in a bright green van, with my parents blasting Michael Jackson songs over the speakers. I couldn't wait to get out. A typical, "too cool for school" teenager, I did the farewell formalities with my parents, and then shuffled into the swarm of the three hundred other 6th, 7th and 8th graders with the same identity crisis. The one thing besides our personal image on our minds was, "What was our schedule?" I wanted to know who would be in each of my classes. Would my best friend Chad Clarke join me again for advanced English? Would I get PE with the friend I played 1 vs 1 basketball with all summer long? I was equally nervous about who my teachers would be. Would I get that teacher that everyone adored- who threw a beach ball around on the first day to help students get to know each other? Or would I get the teacher who was so strict she made three kids cry before 2nd period?

Regardless of the outcome, my schedule was fixed. I had little input about which teachers I got, who my classmates would be, and what classes I would take. Sure, I had choice of my electives; but by the end of the school year, I was required to take the same electives as everybody else in middle school.

Like many kids that age, my favorite classes were the ones outside of the "core" blocks. I took small engines and recalled learning how a piston moved up and down and used combustion to power a motor. I took "America's fringe" as an elective and remember vividly learning about the Beatniks as well as the plight of Irish Americans through a spoken monologue.

Similar to my days as a middle-schooler, students today face a similar dilemma. Students keep their schedules stuffed in the front of their binders to serve as a constant reminder of where they should be, when they should be there, and how many minutes they will spend in each class.

What if scheduling was different? What if rather than building learning around fixed schedules, we built flexible schedules around learning? What if learning experiences in schools were as adaptive and fluid as they are in the world outside of school?

Equipped with our small systems, we **can** make this happen.

Let's return to my earlier premise about the power of small models. Large organizations (schools especially) depend on schedules to organize the thousands of constituents who walk through their doors each day. Without schedules, the large school could not move along a predictable, guaranteed pathway. Schedules help keep and promote a sense of order to guarantee fixed outcomes. But in smaller systems, teachers can have more flexibility in maneuvering the schedule to best fit their students' needs. Scheduling can be a cooperative and collaborative process tailored to promote the best outcomes for each student. Imagine if as a student, rather than take a traditional English class, you took a course with fellow computer junkies entitled, "Literacy through programming." Or if computers weren't your forte, perhaps the course, "Becoming an Amazon Best- Seller" would be more intriguing. Teachers would organize themselves according to the needs of their students and courses they felt most confident in delivering. Perhaps classes would be mixed between grade levels. Rather than grade specific outcomes, the teacher of each course would differentiate the delivery of content to develop the skills of each child.

This of course begs the question of how to arrange such classes and flexible schedules. By no means am I saying that this will be an easy task. However, if you value developing the unique talents and gifts of each child, it is mandatory that you schedule time for developing flexible schedules. Find opportunities in the schedule for shared prep time with fellow members of each department or committee. This collaborative time will help teachers organize content and create a schedule that allows students several choices on how to achieve the desired outcomes. If you are handcuffed by course- specific content, look at a more creative way of delivering common standards.

Flexible Scheduling in a small model

Again, it is no surprise that flexible scheduling works better in smaller systems. Smaller teams can be more agile and responsive to various needs, both of facilitators and students. This was the premise *Futures Academy* was built upon. In its inception, other than a few elective blocks in the middle of the day, it literally had a blank schedule with which to plan around. We were given the same blank paper I presented you with at the onset of this book. It was a gift that few educators have had the luxury to receive. We wanted to treat it delicately.

Being three of the most flexible people in existence, we welcomed the freedom, as we preferred to let things happen organically. And while we realized the importance of outlining and blocking out chunks of time to teach certain content, we didn't want student learning to be mandated by the infallible fixed schedule. We sold Futures Academy on the idea that it would be honed and tailored so specifically to student need, that we would have to work individually with students to build their schedules.

A blank slate stood in front of us, with limitless opportunity for student experiences.

First we decided on the "non-negotiables." No matter how much you tried to convince parents that "writing through rap" was content specific, we understood that parents and the administration felt much more secure seeing a block filled into their student's schedule that read "Humanities."

Therefore, core blocks were our "non-negotiables. It was our way of guaranteeing that despite a very unorthodox mode of delivery, we would still deliver the core content of the curriculum. At the same time however, to follow through on our promise of more individualized learning, we had to allow blocks of time for student passion and learning built around their specific needs. These parts of the schedule included "passion block"- an opportunity for students to learn a new skill unrelated to course specific content; "wellness"- a chunk of time that allowed students to design their own fitness routines or join a physical education class according to their interest; "project block"- a time reserved solely for any project work related to integrated or individualized learning goals; and finally, "mentoring"- a time each morning to build connections and focus on developing the "whole child."

Here is the initial vision we had for scheduling at the inception of Futures Academy, before students even stepped foot in the door:

	Monday	Tuesday	Wednesday	Thursday	Friday
8:00-9:00	Field Inquiry	Mentoring	Mentoring	Mentoring	Mentoring: Schedule Creation
9:00-10:00		Frontloading	Skill Building (Math, Chinese)	Frontloading	Skill Building (Math, Chinese)
10:00-11:00	Project Check-In		Project Action Lab		Project Action Lab
11:00-12:00	Skill Building (Math, Chinese)	Internship			
	Lunch		Lunch	Lunch	Lunch
12:00-1:00	Enrichment		Enrichment	Flexible	Enrichment
13:00-14:00	Flexible				
14:00-15:00	Wellness		Wellness		Project Critique
15:00-16:00		Language Development		Virtual Collaboration	Language Development
16:00-17:00		ASA		ASA	

Little Johnny- A case study

Like many of you, I am a visual learner. And explaining scheduling so pedantically fails to invite you into the magic and impact that flexibility has on student learning. Therefore, I will put you into the shoes of one of our students. For the sake of anonymity, we will call him Johnny. I won't tell you much about Johnny other than the fact that he is a computational genius, lover of robots, fan of tennis, and like many masterminds, painfully awkward and introverted.

Let's take you through an actual Thursday in *Futures Academy* according to Jonny flexible schedule.

Jonny comes to school early, before the sun has fully risen to fuss around with his arduino- the miniature brain able to manipulate small robots. His friend Cliff, who arrives to school early to configure new levels for a video game soon, joins him. Cliff watches some youtube videos to find ideas and transfers the information into a word document to dictate player commands.

Other students begin filing in and taking seats amongst the comfortable furniture around the room. Some sit and discuss the latest teenage gossip on red beanbags while others rock from side to side on specially designed chairs intended to improve student engagement.

Let's return to Johnny. After a brief reminder from the facilitators that mentoring is to start in a minute, Johnny closes his screen and rolls his high-tech "node" chair to a group circle where *Futures Academy* meets at the beginning of each day. Johnny is soon welcomed by the facilitators and the classmates on his right and left through a greeting and follow up sharing a topic. Next, Johnny is asked to close his eyes for the next activity designed to frame student learning for that day. With eyes closed, three students are designated "tappers," responsible for tapping the shoulders of students who embody the characteristics dictated by the facilitators. Johnny manages to crack a grin when he is tapped on the shoulder for being one of the most "innovative" students in the class. It is now his turn to "tap" students who are effective group members. Without a second thought, Johnny moves across the circle to tap the shoulder of a girl who helped configure the design for their Rube Goldberg machine. The activity continues for another five minutes with the final category embodying the class's most effective presenters. Once the final students are tapped, students are asked to open their eyes. Johnny is not one of the four tapped. He listens as the Humanities facilitator clarifies that these last four students will be asked to help lead a middle school-wide "poetry café" conducted by MS Humanities held in the cafeteria; giving students an opportunity to share their favorite poems as well as read their own. It would also establish a foundation for an organic opportunity for Johnny later that day in English class, where he would visit the library and begin analyzing his favorite poem.

Mentoring ends with one of Johnny's classmates reading the school- wide daily announcements and the facilitators giving a brief overview of the day. Johnny is then asked to gather his materials for Humanities while a few of his good friends are asked to gather their supplies for Science, being held on the opposite side of the movable white boards stretched across the room. Facilitators determine the groups based on their project work in each class. In Science, they are in the midst of finishing designs and learning the physics principals behind Rube Goldberg machines, while in Humanities, they are in stage two of an integrated project with Chinese that asks students to experience life from another person's perspective. After Johnny takes his seat, his overly excitable Humanities teacher asks him to observe the symbols on each desk. Each group possesses a symbol for one of the five major world religions. His facilitator explains that ultimately, students will be responsible for understanding how religion impacts their given person's daily life to better cognize how to comprise their "Life in a Day" video; filmed from their global character's perspective. After framing the purpose of the lesson, Johnny is asked to get up and move to the religion that matches each category dictated by his facilitator.

Johnny finds he knows much more about Christianity compared to the other Eastern religions, which is troublesome given his assigned global character is from Tibet. Fortunately, there are a few members in Johnny's small group that also practice Buddhism, and are therefore able to provide some guidance on how religion might impact his life.

Meanwhile, on the other side of the whiteboards dividing the room, Johnny's science facilitator is giving a dynamic lesson in physics, teaching properties of motion so that groups will be more successful in the design of their own Rube Goldberg machines. And while this particular lesson is not integrated with what is happening in Humanities, a flexible schedule allows for Johnny to get more individualized attention and instruction. In fact, after about forty minutes of exploring the affect of religion on daily life, rather than being asked to move to the next class, his facilitators switch places and deliver the same lesson to Johnny's group. And while it's a bit of a stretch, Johnny's Science facilitator can relate forces and motions to the "invisible factors" that influence daily life.

After the blended Math and Humanities block, Johnny takes a short break, where he has the opportunity to mix with the students outside of *Futures Academy*. The "geek squad" as he calls his group of friends is eager to discuss new video games and the nanotechnology they read about in *Popular Science*.

After the break, Johnny returns to class where he finds his classmates huddled in a circle around a blank whiteboard. Johny's facilitator asks students to brainstorm possible activities to complete during their *flexible* block of time; a period for students to catch up on project work, or work towards SMART goals set around each subject. Given Johnny's prolific computational ability, working on Math is less relevant than building his skills in Humanities, specifically related to his vocabulary. While Johnny has been engaged in his current piece of writing in Humanities, it lacks the diversity of word choice to engross the reader. When prompted, Johnny shares "vocabulary development" as a possible activity. Ultimately the board is filled with six sample activities of which to complete during *Flexible Block*.

Having identified a Humanities-related goal, Johnny seeks the support of his Humanities facilitator in consulting the appropriate vocabulary enrichment app. Taking a seat next to him, Johnny's teacher shows Johnny a site called "vocabulary.com;" a vocabulary building site designated to move at the pace of the user. Together, the pair set a realistic goal of how much to complete during the time. After about twenty- five minutes of work on vocabulary enrichment, Johnny takes a self- imposed break to grab some water and fresh air outside. He returns after a few minutes to find his Math facilitator has taken the free seat beside his empty chair. Similar to Humanities, Johnny had recently developed a SMART goal related to Math; which was tough given his current level of mastery. In only a week's time, Johnny would represent the entire school in the "Mathletes" competition. In a typical Math class, the teacher would work to support Johnny in the given curriculum, but certainly struggle to find problems according to his level; Johnny has already mastered the 7th and 8th grade curriculum. Fortunately, Johnny's facilitator has other resources at his disposal. At the beginning of the year, he introduced the whole class to a dynamic and intuitive online tool called "Khan Academy." This free course allowed students to self- direct their learning, moving at a pace appropriate to their level of math mastery. Jonny knew that while his number sense was exceedingly strong, he could always work on his spatial visual skills; a topic crucial to understanding 9th grade Math. After reviewing his progress on the other silos, Johnny entered the course entitled "Manipulating Shapes." Together with his facilitator, they set a goal to complete ten of the introductory problems, which included a brief video tutorial embedded within the course content.

Johnny's flexible block feels like it ended as soon as it began; the most productive ninety minutes of his past week. Dying to get his tech release fix, Johnny joins his friends outside as they explore the quad-copter, *Futures Academy's* new high- tech toy. The robot climbs into the sky as Johnny's friend Timmy mans the controllers a hundred feet below. Studying the flight of the miniature machine, Johnny makes a few mental calculations of gear to motor ratio necessary to give the machine the proper lift. Johnny's Chinese facilitator props his head out the door and gives Johnny a three- minute warning. In only a few minutes, Johnny will be asked to return to class to work on his narrative writing piece connected to the integrated unit with Humanities.

Johnny returns to class, short of breath, to a message on the front screen that prompts him and other "Group B" students to take a seat with nothing but their laptops and an "open mind." Once seated, Johnny's Chinese facilitator explains that this particular lesson would be delivered jointly with Humanities. Before questions can begin, his teacher breaks into a poetic reading of "Walk in My Shoes," a poem intended to develop empathy amongst its readers. Although Johnny struggles to pick out certain words, he can understand the overall theme. For his peers, who have been in China for only a short time, the poem holds no meaning. Johnny's Humanities teacher explains that he will be reading the same poem in English. Johnny's classmates take a collective sigh of relief. When finished with the same reading, students are directed to write down words they heard both in Chinese and English. Stronger Chinese speakers are asked to teach their non-native peers the meaning of the words while the native English speakers are directed to teach the connotations of the English words. After discussing newfound vocabulary, the facilitators refocus student attention to a sidewall where the unit question drapes just beneath the ceiling: *"What's it like to walk in someone else's shoes?"* Facilitators explain that students will be responsible for writing two poems; one from the perspective of their local Chinese home-stay partner and one from a character in a more global setting. Facilitators give students the remaining thirty-five minutes to find a poem related to the main theme that intrigues them.

Let's debrief the power of flexible scheduling on Jonny day.

In less than a half day, Johnny has been able to direct his schedule, experience integrated teaching around a common theme, learn in small skill specific groups, and be part of a collective, shared experience. You too can give students these invaluable experiences by looking at the way you currently schedule and challenging yourself to think differently. While you may not have the same freedoms as *Futures Academy*, you can start by developing common prep time with teachers of different subject levels. Use this time to plan an integrated experience. If it's within the same subject, look for a grade- wide common experience; if it's outside your subject area, look for some organic curricular connections; and if it's outside of your grade level, look for a coaching type of experience, with older students acting as mentors for the content you are responsible for delivering within your grade.

Limit the number of subjects

How many classes does a typical student in your school attend each day? More likely than not, it's too many. If we are to capitalize on the advantages of flexible scheduling, we are going to have to limit the number of classes students take each day. In most schools, students attend at least "three core blocks" and one or two "specialist blocks." That's five lessons a day. According to research on adolescent brains, it takes ten minutes to close and solidify concepts in a lesson and, at least, ten minutes for their brains to readjust to a new lesson. If a student sees five teachers a day, that's a hundred minutes of wasted time! Think of how schools could use that lost time. It's an even harsher adjustment for the teacher who must transition to five new classes with five varying sets of students, all with varying levels of needs.

Instead of scheduling according to guaranteed minutes, we should schedule according to what the learning requires. If students are in the process of creating their small businesses, they will need lots of time with math and social studies to learn the economic principals. Likewise, if they are working with a local cancer research center to find better treatment options, it will necessitate the need for more time with the science teacher to help learn the appropriate chemistry and biology principals. If you are concerned that one subject will be given too much priority through this approach, then map out the entire year with teachers from other departments to ensure you have adequate time to cover your standards. This will foster deeper learning.

Once you have the core subjects covered, consider how you utilize the specialists at your school. Rather than send students to the art and music specialist to learn unrelated content, book these specialists according to the relevance of the learning opportunity. In this way, the specialist classes like Art and Music will be spread throughout the year, and given more weight at the appropriate times. Specialists would be "booked" much like you would book an appointment with a doctor or dentist. After working with the other teachers to plan meaningful units and learning experiences, you would book the most appropriate specialist to help support the plan.

In *Futures Academy*, the specialists have served of monumental importance in enforcing the intended objectives of the unit. For our small business unit, we "booked" the art and music teachers to help students with their business logos and advertising jingles. Rather than require students to attend both classes as part of a fixed schedule, students signed up for the Arts classes that interested them the most. In the end, instead of students seeing two specialists a week for a short lesson, unrelated to bigger picture learning goals, they were able to see the same specialist twice and learn content relevant to the larger learning goals.

Flexible scheduling will allow you to foster deeper connections with content and integrate learning in a way that makes sense. It will also become a collaborative process that involves small interdependent teams.

Where to start with flexible scheduling

If you are ready to take the plunge into trying flexible scheduling yourself, I would suggest you start by mapping out the learning you want to achieve and brainstorm blocks of time that will allow you to achieve these outcomes. Get together with an integrated team of teachers across multiple subject areas and develop goals as an integrated team. This will ensure that blocks of time are not prescribed according to subjects, but rather by deeper learning opportunities. Here are some that we came up with before creating the schedule in *Futures Academy:*

- Wellness Block

- Self- Directed Learning Block

- Virtual Collaboration Block

- Project Block

- Skill Building Block

Note how the blocks above include a range of subjects, learning opportunities and experiences for students. Determining how to fill each block will be dictated by the demands of the integrated unit.

Flexible Scheduling within a large school

Again, I cannot overstate the importance of organizing scheduling in a way that supports the learning, rather than tailor learning around the fixed schedule. I will give you an example of this principal in the context of our very large International School of Beijing. Humanities teachers met during common planning time to look at the content standards they were responsible for covering over the remainder of the year. Knowing that we had a famous "slam poet" visiting the school for two weeks in early Spring, we decided to organize course content according to this organic connection, despite the fact that poetry and narrative writing was originally planned for later in the year. In addition, rather than deliver a uniform course on "poetry" and how to find your voice,

Humanities teachers organized several workshops according to the type of poetry they were most passionate in delivering. The result was a plethora of options for how students would learn the valuable writing lessons of poetry, either through odes, limericks, haiku, "found poetry," or my personal favorite and the seminar I led, poetry through "Rock n' Roll!"

Were we all responsible for the same content? Yes. Were we hoping to achieve similar outcomes? Of course. Was the course content delivered in the same way? No. Similar to flexible scheduling, we had to organize our workshops according to our individual passions and student needs.

What part of the schedule will you have control over? Perhaps it's only a few short blocks of time. If so, step outside your comfort zone and collaborate with that gregarious drama teacher down the hall, especially if you know she is one of the teachers receiving your kids later in the day. Regardless of where you teach or what your schedule dictates, we all have the power to make small changes to make learning more meaningful and relevant for our students.

The poetry seminars were not an isolated instance of flexible scheduling. They represented one of several attempts by teachers to make learning more relevant and integrated for their students. A later, more sustainable example of flexible scheduling came during the eighth- grade Humanities unit on *revolutions*. In studying various revolutions, teachers hoped students would gain the key concepts of governmental systems and factors that led to revolt. Rather than study each revolution or skim over the surface of several to deliver key content, teachers elected instead to deliver three-week mini- units on revolutions according to student interest. These in- depth studies allowed teachers to not only meet shared outcomes but also boost student engagement in the process. In the end, I asked the teachers if it was difficult to rearrange student schedules to allow for this opportunity. Cleary empowered by this new way of thinking, many of them insisted that it was actually easier to arrange scheduling in such a way.

Flexible Blocks for 21ˢᵗ Century Learning

The following represents a list of additional ways in which you might create structured yet flexible time in the 21ˢᵗ Century:

- **Integrated Block:** This allocated block of time allows for integrated learning around a common theme. It can include:

  o *Project Time:* This is time for students to work towards deadlines for their integrated project. It is different from passion project in that the time is more structured around collective learning goals.

  o *Current Events around a "Big Idea":* Take a "big idea" in the news which may include:

    Economic Crisis

    Conflict that affects the whole world

  o *Global Issue Discussion:* Unlike the current event blocks of time, these blocks focus around wider issues that have no immediate solution. Issues like "Women's Rights;" "Poverty;" "Global Warming."

- **Team Teaching Block:** This is a block of time to deliver instruction with a partner teacher, preferably in another subject. Together, you deliver the important concepts built around whatever issue or topic it is you are exploring.

- **Passion Project Block**: This block of time is part of a semester-long project where students determine their area of passion, and work closely with a chosen mentor to complete a related project. Here are some examples:

  o Write a novel series

  o Build a student library for students in need

  o Come up with a small business that serves the community

  o Fuse new foods together and serve in a "student restaurant"

- **Self- Directed Flex Block:** This is a block of time where students direct their learning. This is perhaps the most flexible block of time we have offered and involves the student identifying their objective at the beginning of the period, and the facilitator checking in at the end to confirm that they reached their goal.

- **Reader's/ Writer's Workshop Block**: This time is for reader's/ writer's workshop. Start with a mini-lesson and build the crucial concepts around the writing of the student's choosing.

- **Learning Lab Block:** This block of time is reserved for small "lab" like sessions that students sign up for in advance. Ensure at least a few days in between the time students sign up and the time in which you deliver the labs to provide the most impactful learning for your students.

- **Buddy Block**: This is a time to work collectively with students and teachers in other sectors of the school. After forging a relationship with another classroom, provide each of your students a "buddy." Determine what activities you will structure in with your buddy class.

Flexibility vs. Structure

I cannot overstate the importance of balancing flexible timetabling with some fixed structures. Flexible scheduling as mentioned previously has not been one smooth ride from start to finish. The very idea rests on the important presupposition that students can direct and chart their learning paths and that facilitators are equipped with the training to help support them in getting there. Can they? Of course. Might students and facilitators need some help? Definitely. Therefore, if you are to be successful with reconfiguring schedules and allotting time according to the demands of the learning experience, it is first important to establish regular structures for feedback, clarity, and forecasting what those flexible blocks of time will look like. This next section will help in establishing those daily routines.

Mentoring- A practical way to establish structure

Some call it homeroom, others call it "academic coaching," and even more call it mentoring. Whatever name you give it, this period of time can help establish a solid foundation for the learning experiences that will happen throughout the day. This time has been crucial for *Futures Academy* in helping to discuss the outcomes of learning throughout the day in addition to providing the structures necessary for the self- directed tasks students will pursue. We first spend time greeting each other, transition to a brief guiding question activity to set the context for the day and then spend critical time reviewing or creating the schedule for the day. For our more methodical students, it allows them to prepare academically and mentally, and for our more free- spirits, it sets some boundaries for undertakings they choose to pursue. Often, unforeseeable events like school visits, experiential learning opportunities, and spontaneous creative ideas present themselves, which of course we are still able to adapt to; but by mapping out a general outline for the day, we can ensure certain targets are met.

Getting it Right

I want to discuss the evolution of flexible scheduling in Futures Academy to demonstrate that scheduling is **tricky** and that it takes time to get it right.

It would be dishonest if I told you that as facilitators, we understood how to implement flexible scheduling from the onset. We all came from schools in which schedules were prescribed. And as free thinking as we were with our initial scheduling, after some trial, and as the program grew in size, we soon confined ourselves to the same narrow thinking that constricted the schools we came from. Like you, we had our doubts about **all** students becoming self- directed learners. Perhaps we did not create enough clear guidelines about utilizing their time; or perhaps we as facilitators were overwhelmed with the amount of freedom they had. Whatever the case, this was what the schedule looked like at the onset of *Futures Academy's* second year, with 70 students spread across two grade levels.

	Day 1		Day 2		Day 3		Day 4		Day 5		Day 6	
Mentoring 8:15-8:35	MENTORING		MENTORING		MENTORING		MENTORING		MENTORING		MENTORING	
Block A 8:35-10:00	Humanities		Science		Humanities A / Science A		Humanities B / Science B		Wellness A / Math, Passion		Wellness B / Math, Passion	
Break 10:00-10:15												
Block B 10:15-11:35	Wellness A	Flexible Chinese / English	Wellness B	Flexible Chinese / English	Chinese	Math	Health		Humanities	Chinese	Flexible	
Block C 11:40-12:25	Enrichment		Enrichment		Enrichment		Enrichment		Enrichment		Enrichment	
MS Lunch 12:25-13:10												
Block D 13:10-13:55	Group 2 Chinese	Writing/ Reading	Group 1 Chinese	Writing/ Reading	Group 2 Chinese	Writing/ Reading	Group 1 Chinese	Writing/ Reading	Group 2 Chinese	Writing/ Reading	Group 1 Chinese	Writing/ Reading
Block E 14:00-15:25	Humanities	Math	Project Block		Wellness A / Passion		Math / Wellness B / Passion		Math	Writing &Reading (French +Band)	Project Block	

Overwhelming right? Doesn't exactly look like a schedule that would promote self- directed learning and flexible thinking does it? In fact, the *Futures Academy* schedule looked even more prescriptive than the schedule of the larger school of which it was a part. And while we were still doing many of the innovative things we promised as the cornerstones of the program, we were confined by this iteration. Like predecessors before us, we began equating learning with the amount of time it was provided in the schedule.

As is the case with any new program, it has taken us some time to get things right. And while we would never claim to have perfected the concept of flexible scheduling, we believe that now, midway through year two of the program's development, we have aligned flexible scheduling with the Academy's vision. In a way, scheduling has come back full circle- starting out free and unconstrained; moving into more structure and confinement; and back to the free and unconstrained qualities from which it began. We now have the confidence that we do not have to pencil in designated times for each subject to ensure learning, but rather large blocks of time to offer the kind of deep, integrated experiences that the learning requires. Here is our current Futures Academy schedule:

Sample Schedule

Grade 7	DAY A	DAY B	DAY C	
	Mentoring	Mentoring	Mentoring	
Period 1	Integrated (math priority)	Integrated	Math A	RWWS B
Period 2	PE Option/ Flex	Integrated	Math B	RWWS A
Period 3 Period 4	Language/ Enrichment	Language/ Enrichment	Language/ Enrichment	
Period 5	Art	Passion Learning Lab	PE	

	DAY D	DAY E	DAY F	
	Mentoring	Mentoring	Mentoring	
Period 1	Integrated	PE	Integrated	
Period 2	Integrated	Math B	RWWS A	Integrated
Period 3 Period 4	Language/ Enrichment	Language/ Enrichment	Language/ Enrichment	
Period 5	Art	Math A	RWWS B	Passion Learning Lab

Key:

Integrated: Block built around the needs of the project. Includes front loading, team teaching and project work time.

Language/ Enrichment: Block for foreign language or enrichment, which acts as an elective, giving students over thirty choices.

RWWS: Reading and writer's workshop

Flex: Flexible block designed around student choice

Learning Lab: Students write goals and direct learning. Facilitators to offer 1 on 1 support.

Passion: Two short blocks throughout the week where students have time to work on a project related to their passion. Acts much like "Google Time."

Math A/B: Math block to build and support skills necessary for the project. Individualized.

From the students

The students have appreciated the changes we have made to the schedule to make it more flexible and built around their needs. And not surprisingly, they have been able to identify exactly how it has impacted their learning. Here are a few of their comments in regards to our current schedule:

"The best feature of Futures Academy so far is that we have a very flexible class. We have flexible timetables so that we can always adjust our time. Also, during class, we can do projects that are of our interest." - John, grade 7

"I like the periods that the normal classes don't have: Learning Lab, Passion Project, and Integrated. It helps us learn more efficiently." - Sally, grade 7

"I think one of the best features of FA so far is its flexible schedules and connections between the subjects." - Mark, grade 7

"We have more free time to work on our designated problem/homework, so we don't have anything for later." - Jessica, grade 7

In Closing

Not all of you have the same luxury as we did in developing flexible schedules. Some of you have class sizes of over thirty students and a rigorous curriculum to deliver. Time may be even more confining as it has given you very little opportunity to offer the kind of integrated experiences outlined above. But remember, this is about doing what you can, slowly transforming your school one small step at a time.

At the end of the day, as always, you decide the amount of flexibility you introduce within the schedule. As is the case with any big change, it is best to chart the waters carefully before diving in headfirst: Some of the changes I introduced were great while others were minor tweaks. However, let's return to the initial purpose of this section; making learning more relevant to the demands of the future through flexible scheduling. By removing the confining structure of a fixed schedule, you have been able to make monumental changes. You have opened up the opportunities for integrated, authentic learning opportunities while also fostering organic connections with other teachers, grade levels, and course content. You have sought out and delivered upon organic connections to the real world. The next section will capitalize on the changes you have already made while extending possibilities by looking at how you configure space.

Flexible Space

Perhaps the most cliché phrase of the rapidly evolving 21st Century is the claim that educators must prepare "students for jobs that do not even exist." This catch phrase has seeped its way into many schools, institutions of higher learning, and into the mantra and psyche of every teacher dedicated to developing their craft. And yet, few of us have done anything about it. Sure, we have made minor changes, generalizing curriculum to more conceptual aims, transitioning the old "No Child Left Behind" standards to the new "Common Core," or offering alternative routes to learning via online classes and project- based learning, but we've still kept the same underlying structures. Students still enter new classrooms to acquire content disconnected from the one they just left behind, or receive number grades from a new "state of the art" reporting system that in essence does no more than replicate the grading system of the past.

You see, as much as schools would like to change at the same pace as surrounding society, few are courageous enough to do away with the structures they know are holding students back. The archaic structure I would like us to remove in this section is the traditional classroom.

Let's return to the blank piece of paper that stood in front of you at the beginning of this book. For lack of a better title, let's call it your "classroom." Regardless of where we teach or what school and district we are a part of, most of us have been given a space to deliver our course content. While they differ in size, these "classroom" spaces typically look the same from school to school: a space enclosed by four walls, two exits, a few windows, a teacher desk, student desks with chairs, some white board space and built in places for technology.

"Upgrading" these spaces to the 21st century usually involves talks about "Smartboards," "1 to 1" laptops, or other technological innovations designed to expedite the process of teaching and learning. And while these changes have most certainly benefited the speed and effectiveness of learning, they have not brought about the kind of systemic change necessary to propel schooling into the 21st Century. Schooling needs a new narrative for classroom design that I believe starts and ends with flexible space.

In order to start the dialogue around flexible space, I'm going to ask you a question that is going to encourage you to think differently:

"What's your purpose in the classroom?"

Rather than start by restructuring space, we need to first start by determining the purpose the space serves. Think back to the vision statement you wrote at the beginning of this book. What's your sticking point as an educator? This is what will guide you in configuring your space. Is your main purpose as a classroom teacher to foster collaboration between your students? Is your main purpose to help students connect content? Is your main purpose to create inquirers and inspire curiosity?

Take some time to really think this through. Before the onset of the Internet or advanced technology, these were much easier questions to answer. Twenty to thirty years ago, teachers represented the bridge between our students and success. Attending school and universities of higher education were clearly linked to success and there was a plethora of statistics to support their necessity. College graduates on a whole experienced greater salaries and success than those without a degree. Those who attended university, because of a Liberal Arts Education, were more likely to become involved citizens in their communities and counties. School for the most was compulsory, relevant and a gateway to success in the real world.

In 2015 however, schools are not such clear pathways to success. For every compulsory class in college, there is an equivalent online alternative for only a fraction of the cost. For every skill that takes six months of schooling to complete, there are Youtube tutorials able to deliver the same learning in six short programs. For every IVY league school touting to connect your idea to the investment money necessary to get it off the ground, there are crowd- source funding platforms that allow your idea to be funded right away.

Therefore, as educators, we have to create a space that accommodates for this new mode of learning. We are no longer deliverers of the core content but rather facilitators of learning, able to encourage students to ask the right questions and seek out the appropriate answers. Here's another question we must ask ourselves:

Where does "school" exist in the "real world?"

Name one thing that looks like school in the real world. Does any structure in the real world have guaranteed outcomes? What place in the real world can tell you exactly what you will be doing in the future, when you will be doing it, and for how long? Perhaps in the industrial age this was the case, but in the rapidly advancing 21st century, outcomes are flexible and ever-changing. Our classrooms must reflect this reality.

Finding the answers

Let's answer our first question: What is our purpose in the classroom?

Our purpose in the 21st Century as teachers is to facilitate learning. We are not the "sages on stage" or the grand disseminators of knowledge, but rather the "guides on the sides;" coaches

38

responsible for asking the right questions and helping students seek out, connect and find the answers themselves. Once we can accept this role, it is quite easy to see how to configure classroom space to fulfill this aim.

A classroom with no fixed front.

As a facilitator of learning, there should be no clear front to your classroom. Your class should be set up in a configuration that allows for multiple learning spaces, with no established hierarchy. Students should be able to move around freely to a multitude of activities that help them explore the topic of study. With multiple classroom "fronts," several types of learning can happen congruently. Small groups can work in a Socratic format on a given topic while others can analyze reading passages on soft seats in the corner.

Make thinking visible.

How do you make thinking visible in your classroom? Remember our premise of simplicity that I established in the first section? How might you make student thinking more visible as they progress through their learning journey?

Let's take a traditional Humanities lesson to demonstrate the antithesis to this idea before developing its key components. Students begin with a quick- write to frame their minds around learning that day, debrief with a partner, hear a short lecture exposing them to more content, complete a small group activity, and then reflect at the end of the lesson via an exit ticket or journal post. While this kind of learning was certainly of value to the student, the facilitator had few archival indicators of student achievement.

What if you could know what students were thinking at all times?

To achieve this aim, you have to make thinking visible. Purchase tables with "writable" surfaces. Rather than brainstorm via a laptop or journal, students can brainstorm what they already know directly on the surface of their table. Place large poster paper on the side walls, pose a central question to the learning and ask students to document their responses. The sharing and dissemination of these ideas can occur via a gallery walk. As the facilitator for learning, you can circulate the room to see what common misconceptions exist. In this way, conversations in the classroom can start around student thoughts and ideas.

If budgets or administration will not support the purchase of writable surfaces, make them on your own. Take laminate from the copy room and affix it to the tops of each table surface. Or, after measuring the surface area of each tabletop, make a trip down to the local hardware store and purchase white tag board to nail to each desk. This transformation will carry a very inexpensive price tag compared to the overall benefit it will have in making thinking more visible within your classroom.

Finally, if the thought of students writing on tables makes your blood boil, use tech tools like Google Docs, Microsoft OneNote, "popplets," or other software that allow for multiple access points at the same time. In this way, information will be consolidated while also allowing students to learn and gain from each other.

The *Futures Academy Space* is filled with whiteboard space. Students can write on every table and movable wall in whatever color they please, just as long as it relates to the learning. We generally conduct brainstorms at the onset of any new unit or concept and ask students to document their thinking directly on the surfaces. In small groups, students can see similar thinking patterns, find areas of disagreement, and finally and most importantly, use these ideas to foster more ideas of their own. Pictured below you will see students brainstorming story starters for their creative writing pieces.

Writable Surfaces

Transparency

If you are making learning visible from within the classroom, why not also make it visible from outside? I bet many of you teach in spaces that are rarely observed. A supervisor might visit with you two to three times a year and parents may come to back to school night and a few exhibitions scattered throughout units of study, but in general, you are pretty isolated from the outside world. It's time to change that.

We all know the value of observation in improving our practice and need to become more comfortable with people interacting with our space. If you have windows, purchase a cheap set of blinds that open and close from above your windows. In this way, you can easily make the space observable from the outside while also allowing for the privacy of a more intimate lesson. For those of you who teach in obscure wings of the school where reclusive insects won't visit, request to deliver instruction in a space more visible. I bet if you took an inventory of available space in the school, you would find that there is more open space than you might have previously imagined. Get creative. How about that multi-purpose room that is only used for large presentations five to six times a year? Or the computer lab that occupies 50 square meters of space in the center of the school. If we are going to change the way we think and teach, we've got to place ourselves in a more visible wing of the school.

Futures Academy model of transparency

You will not find any fixed walls in the entire Futures Academy Space. What divides the large 1,000 square meter space? Movable partitions. As seamless as it was to make the space open, we can easily confine it if breaking out into small group activities. The one commonality is that regardless of how we configure our fluid space, it will always be observable from the outside.

The area sits in the epicenter of the school. If every road in 3rd Century led to Rome, every road in our massive four- story school leads to *Futures Academy*. There is no hiding. That's because the space sits adjacent to the hallway that receives the most foot traffic in the school. Rather than wall us in, we installed glass from floor to ceiling to act as a fishbowl and incubator for great ideas. If teachers, administrators or visitors wish to observe a lesson or activity, they have merely to place their face against the glass or step down three stairs into our space. If we are to promote transparency, we must model it first.

How does this transform practice?

The implications for best practice are boundless with this level of transparency. You would hardly want to save lesson planning for the last minute in this high stakes environment. By exposing yourself to those outside, you have added an extra level of integrity to your work. The next step is to invite other teachers to act as critical friends for your work. Rather than wait for your supervisor to visit twice a year, ask teachers from the same department to observe and offer feedback. This will both foster collaboration and transform the culture of teaching at your school. Your openness will inspire others to be equally transparent in their facilitating of instruction.

An integrated office space

Where do you do most of your lesson planning? Chances are you work from within your classroom or in an adjacent office that houses at most two people. If we are to make learning more clear and visible, we are going to have to change the way in which we plan. I would start by requesting that your administrator replaces your shared wall with one that slides open and closes along a movable track. This will make co- teaching far more achievable and will mark the first step towards greater collaboration. In regards to office space, I suggest inviting another teacher to share your space. In this way, you will be encouraged to discuss ideas while also being able to step in and out during class time.

Movable Partition

Shared Office Space

Grouping of Tables

If you still have large wooden desks that should have been banned in the 50's, do not worry- you are in good company. I used to teach in a classroom with old, heavy wooden furniture that required, at least, two students to lift; one on each end. If this reflects your situation, I can only empathize and offer some small suggestions. First, cut a tennis ball in half and place them on the bottoms of each table leg, and chair. This will allow you to move the furniture without causing too much back pain.

If you have a supportive administration and deeper pocket, ask that they purchase trapezoid tables for your classroom. These shapes are easy to manipulate into multiple configurations depending on the activity you have planned.

Grouping of Tables

Create a classroom that promotes inquiry

Perhaps the greatest question you must ask yourself is, "What kind of thinking do you want to promote in your classroom?" With a bit of foresight, you can ensure that your classroom supports the thinking patterns you intend to inspire.

When designing Futures Academy, we were given few limits. An open, dynamic and thematic based curriculum allowed us to have an equally flexible space in which to deliver the learning. One of our initial tasks was finding a space that would allow for the kind of flexibility we knew promoted the 21st century thinking patterns. But we didn't want to custom fit pre-existing classroom space. If, as we stipulated earlier, current learning spaces were indeed poorly adapted to the demands of a more elusive age, we would have to create our own.

At first, plans were far-reaching. There were talks of building an "all weather" space in the courtyards connecting various wings of the school. An unused outdoor space atop a first floor roof was presented as another alternative. However, one of the key tenets of the 21st Century design we intended to promulgate was the transparency amongst key stakeholders; the first two proposed spaces were in isolated pockets of the school.

We were going to have to compromise.

And that's when our director got really creative, stepping completely outside of the box of traditional school design. Staring down into the vast expanse of the library, he stood transfixed by the possibilities. Could such a staple of the "old world" way of educating also represent the greatest pioneer for change? If indeed, we were going to transform a school, we had to respect its most sacred institution. We imagined the future of learning perched directly above the literary relics of our past. The library was at the epicenter of our school; the structural vortex where the hallways of Middle School, High School and Elementary School met; a large glassed atrium designed to capture light from the outside and disseminate it amongst the learners who sat within. It was the perfect location for Futures Academy and represented what my students and I would soon call "home."

Rather than task local design firms with the responsibility of designing and configuring the space, I wanted the students, our end users and biggest consumers of our product to plan out Futures Academy's interior. They would decide on the furniture, designs for each room, the supporting tech components, and the overall layout. In short, they would utilize the "design-based thinking" process canonized by Stanford to plan out our space. This design cycle is depicted below.

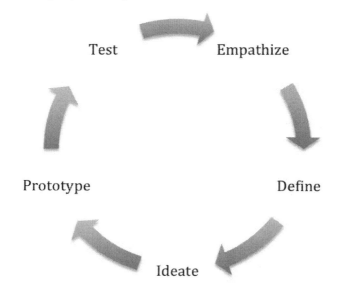

As the facilitator of this process, all I needed to provide were the supporting structures. I provided them with an overall budget, pointed them in the direction of some innovative design firms, put them in contact with our business office, and asked them to consider what the 21st century classroom looked like. We had a tech team, responsible for modernizing the visual, audio and digital setup of the classroom; "interior designers," responsible for dictating overall color scheme, furniture orders and table setup, "design lab dummies" responsible for researching several design lab setups and sketching out the overall layout of our own, and finally, "office staff" responsible for setting up the first kid managed meeting rooms.

As is the case with kids, they immediately gravitated to extremes. Knowing that our intended space was the second floor of the library, they insisted we have a slide to reach the first floor. On a similar vein, rather than move fluidly between classes and blocks of time, they insisted we bounce on balls, and that facilitators wheel around their carts to accommodate student need for a fixed space. And while some of their ideas were indeed outlandish and carried no intent of follow through, they did have a point. Learning spaces should be fluid and designed with the end user in mind.

Nevertheless, I needed to direct them back to our purpose.

I helped filter their ideas into a more practical analysis and discussion of the ultimate goal of the space. Was the cost of spiraling slides worth the benefit it brought to the learning space? Although most of our students had just celebrated their eleventh birthdays, they were wise enough to understand the reasoning behind this basic business principle.

After meeting with Steelcase, a Beijing firm for 21st Century furniture design, students found existing products for their ideas. They worked in small teams to prototype the appropriate configurations and accumulate the costs to ensure it fit within our overall budget.

The result of the three- week design cycle was an amateur exhibition for prospective parents to demonstrate what they could expect should they sign their children up for the program. In short, it served its purpose. Students took what began as unrealistic, non "real-world" ideas and transformed them into integrated solutions. You see, this was a real world with high stakes that existed outside of the traditional curriculum, as the eventual outcome certainly involved the students themselves.

How might you involve students in designing your flexible space?

You might start with an imaginative activity and videotape the process. Place all the existing furniture; bookcases, chairs, tables, desks, etc. against a back wall and write a simple prompt on one of the whiteboards.

"Organize the room in a way that you like."

Students may hesitate at first as the assignment is certainly more open-ended than ones they have been previously exposed to; but give it a few minutes, and I guarantee they will take action. Disagreements will arise, certain students will disengage, a few leaders will emerge, and in short, things will happen. The result will certainly be far different from what you may have envisioned in creating the experience.

I tried this very simulation in the more traditional classroom where I began my educational career. When the simulation concluded, some tables were grouped together in pods of four while others stood off to the side; an even greater part of the room was organized with tables in perfect rows while beanbags lined the exterior amongst the plants and posters. Several posters were removed from the wall as the more organized students insisted that they were distracting and prevented them from focusing. Those posters were then moved to the more colorful section of the room that included posters, natural light, and potted plants. This was the learning environment most conducive for my little "naturalists."

This is what is meant by flexible space. When is the last time you reconfigured the space in your room? Have you asked for student input? Imagine the ownership students would feel over their learning if giving them a chance to design their own space. It would transform the culture of your classroom by signaling your willingness to share in the decision-making process.

From the students

As is always the case with major changes, we must continually ask ourselves if they have impacted students. We had a vision in reconfiguring our space, but would only feel satisfied if students could also identify how the space had impacted their learning. We conducted surveys at three points throughout the year to capture their feedback and see if the space truly made a difference. The surveys were open-ended, asking students to identify what they liked most about Futures Academy. Here are a few of their responses in regards to space:

"The classroom is good for learning. The space has everything we need and the furniture can be moved to suit what we need."- Yumi, grade 7

"I like how different FA is from all the other classes. We have the same space just for FA and all we need to do is to go up a few stairs to get to another class." - Bobby, grade 7

In closing

You are now equipped with several strategies with which to impact student learning. Your clear vision has allowed you to specify the way in which you configure time and space to best reach your students. Rather than organize learning around a fixed schedule that is unadaptable to the demands of the learning, you have organized the schedule in collaboration with others to best fit the demands of the learning experience and the needs of your students. Similarly, you have configured your space to allow you to be a facilitator of learning. Multiple groupings, the re-arrangement of furniture, and an ethos of transparency has inspired other teachers to do the same. The next section will help you build upon what you have learned about flexibility and use it to integrate learning around a common theme.

CHAPTER THREE

INTEGRATED LEARNING

"If you see a whole thing- it seems that it's always beautiful.
Planets, lives...But close up a world's all dirt and rocks."
– Ursula K. Le Guin

Integrated Learning

As a small kid, I had a few peculiarities. When walking to school, I made certain I never stepped on a crack. When given a baseball bat, I would hit pinecones over the fence and imagine that I was in a home run derby contest. I used to sell lemonade to make believe customers on our rural street and do impressions in front of the full body mirror in my shared bedroom. But perhaps most peculiar of all was my inability to get even a minute of sleep without the constant hum of the ceiling fan. This was a problem. My dad hated the ceiling fan. Not because of its appearance or the sound it emitted, after all, he was the one who installed it, but because it was the one appliance responsible for hiking up the electricity bill.

He knew I needed it to sleep, but he also knew that if it ran all night, 7 nights a week, and 30 nights a month, he would have no money left in his bank account. So we made a pact. I could keep the fan in the room under the condition that the minute I fell asleep; the fan switched off. If not, I would be responsible for the associated energy costs. Excited at the prospect of a new mini- project for myself, I shook hands with my dad, and got to work immediately.

My first question was: *Do they sell timers for ceiling fans?* After a bit of research, I discovered that timers did exist, but for a pretty hefty price- at least in my mind. C'mon guys, this was the 80's and my sole source of income was the $3 a week provided me by my parents upon completion of all my chores. I immediately scratched this option.

Option #2: Become aware of my sleep cycle and shut the fan off right before I go into deep REM. I installed a camera the next night and analyzed the tapes. To be expected, after reviewing the tapes, while it was obvious I turned over a few times, without a distinct snoring pattern, there was no way to determine when I *actually* fell asleep.

It seemed I was running out of viable options. And then it dawned on me- I needed to invent something that had not yet been created. But where would I go for help? A year ago, I had literally fallen in love with a VHS series entitled "Mr. McGee." Diligently, I borrowed a new episode each week from my church's bookstore. The series was a cartoon narrated by a mad scientist named Mr. McGee, who followed a young inventor as he came up with solutions to some of the most common problems. There was the vacuum cleaner that never clogged, the 3-d glasses capable of navigating life in three dimensions, and other more complex machines designed to fulfill simple daily tasks. As I watched the videos, I realized that each concept relied on a simple premise: The ingenuity of new ideas relied less on the talent of the inventor and more on looking at problems from a different angle. The program built my confidence in innovative thinking, and I immediately applied the thinking to my unique situation with the ceiling fan.

There was a switch that controlled the fan above my head. The problem was that the switch was located adjacent to the door, close to ground level; while my bed was a perched on a second story loft. Somehow I had to get the light switch to shut off before I fell asleep. While the camera I installed had not given definitive evidence of the time it took to fall asleep, I was pretty sure I could fall asleep within thirty minutes. A timer from our kitchen would ensure I had enough time. If I set the time to thirty minutes, I would be fast asleep by the timer finished its cycle. All I needed to discover now was how to somehow get the light switch off.

In my dad's office, I found the answer. I asked if I could borrow a few of his file folders to help solve the "electricity" crisis along with some scotch tape. He obliged. I cut each manila folder in half, rolled them into tubes, and linked them together with scotch tape. When the tube was long enough to reach from the timer on my bed to the light by the door, there was only one component left to purchase- A small ball. Being a big fan of labyrinth- an engaging game that tests your hand eye coordination, I removed the metal ball from the inner housing, and set up the final product.

The first ten attempts failed. The ball got stuck in the tubing. There wasn't enough force generated to actually turn a switch. The timer was too loud. I hadn't fallen asleep sometimes before the device sprang into action. But these small setbacks were to be expected; after all, it took Thomas Edison nearly one hundred attempts to invent the light bulb. I stuck with it. Eventually, I had a solution to the electricity problem, and even better, a ticket to a good night's sleep.

What's the point of this story? It's definitely not to convince you that inventions like these will advance us in the future, or that my solution pushed the envelope of ingenuity and divergent thinking. The point of the story is to demonstrate the power of integrating learning around a simple concept. In this case, it was getting a fan to turn off and on. Finding a solution meant seeking out other innovations. It meant learning more about the concept of electricity, and principles of forces and motion.

What if school was structured in such a way? What possibilities might exist? What if rather than write curriculum around single subject goals, curriculum writers and teachers alike looked at ways to make learning interconnected? What if learning in school reflected the same principals as learning in the real world; from a genuine "need to know." In my case with the ceiling fan, I needed to know how certain principles worked in order to solve the problem of energy waste. Similarly, classrooms and school should be structured by their relevance in helping solve real world pursuits. Units should derive from relevant questions that engage learners in the process of discovery.

I bet if you sat down with another teacher outside of your subject specific area, you would find multiple ways in which to connect content. You could start with your standards and see what common themes emerge; or from the overall goals of the curriculum; or finally, from major strands or "big ideas."

We used this "big idea" approach in determining the themes for the *Futures Academy curriculum*. Starting integrated units from this common theme allowed us to ensure the most learning across subject areas. For example, when laying out the required content from end to end, my colleagues and I discovered that we were both responsible for covering the concept of "balance." In science, students were required to understand the importance of balance within an ecosystem and food web; and in Social Studies, students were responsible for identifying and explaining the need for balance between a country's foreign and domestic policy. If the most we did was develop the idea that we would teach the next unit through a "balance" lens, we would do more for students than we had done in the past. But, in the end, we would merely scratch the surface of integration.

Again, let's return to the initial reason you picked up this book. You identified yourself as a change agent- someone who rather than shy away from limitless possibility embraces it on a daily basis. I would challenge us all to take the same approach to the idea of integration. Integration should not be confined solely to the demands of our curriculum. It should also include connections we make to businesses that surround the school; nearby villages and communities that send their students to our classes every day; and institutions of higher education blessed with large endowments to pursue this kind of work.

But we need help. We can't pursue this kind of work in isolation and be the only educators willing to leave the shores to set sail in the 21ˢᵗ Century. We need a guiding framework and the knowledge that this kind of integration already exists. Well, I've got great news. It does. Integrated project based learning has been around for over a decade; it's just that very few educators have had the courage, support, or guidance to take those first steps in heeding its lessons. They need a framework and a few willing staff members to join them on the journey. That's where you come in.

Perhaps by explaining the approach *Futures Academy* has taken to integrate learning, it might inspire some ideas of your own, and get you outside of your four walls.

Teaming structures that promote integration

As mentioned in the previous chapters, the most authentic integration occurs in the context of smaller systems. In its second year of implementation, *Futures Academy* has only seven teachers spread across two grade levels. Each grade level consists of two "core teachers" responsible for delivering the core content; one in Math/ Science and one in Humanities. Spread across the two grade levels, that's four core teachers. And because math is a very skills- based discipline and oftentimes a tricky subject to integrate, there is an additional facilitator solely responsible for math content between 7th and 8th grade. The other two facilitators are responsible for language development, the experiential learning opportunities and integration of our program in its context of China. The staffing of Futures Academy is detailed below:

7th Grade	8th Grade
Math/ Science Facilitator	Humanities Facilitator
Humanities Facilitator	Math/ Science Facilitator
Chinese Facilitators	Chinese Facilitators
Math Facilitator	

Futures Academy teams meet every day of the week. Three days of the week are designated as grade level meeting times while the other two are designated for whole team discussions. This ensures both the integration of content within the grade level and within the whole program.

Structuring Integrated Curriculum

In structuring our curriculum, *Futures Academy* facilitators begin by identifying common cross-curricular themes. These would live highest in terms of project development as they had the potential to ensure the most authentic connection between content and subject- specific disciplines. After looking at your own curriculum, look at what themes emerge. If you have the privilege and responsibility of starting integrated planning with no clear guiding framework, do some research and see what themes emerge in the most innovative institutions. I bet you will find some common threads. Here are some common themes to integrate learning around:

- Balance
- Change
- Discovery
- Form
- Conflict
- Identity
- Sustainability
- Relationships
- Time, Place and Space
- Empathy

The themes highlighted in yellow represent the themes that *Futures Academy* identified as allowing for the most authentic integration;

and ones in which we could explore as the program evolved from year to year. Here are the themes and projects that span the two grade levels of Futures Academy.

7th Grade	8th Grade
Identity: Identity Book < ------ >	***Interactions:*** Pecha Kucha Presentation
Systems: Phoenix Project < ------ >	***Discovery:*** Evolution of Knowledge
Rube Goldberg Mini- Project	***Perspective:*** Design a Future Human Capstone Project Introduced
Change: Entrepreneurship < ------ >	***Change:*** Future Societies
Impact: Project Blue Sky < ------ >	***Impact:*** Think Globally/ Act Locally

By maintaining the same themes, we were able to ensure continuity as students move from grade to grade. Rather than vertically articulate around a fixed standard based document, schools can ensure students are building upon their learning with each passing year. This is a fluid process and reflects learning in the real world. You too can create this kind of continuity for students. If you have not been given the same freedom to integrate your curriculum across subject areas, integrate within the same subject but across grade levels. When meeting with your department, rather than discuss each teacher's responsibility in regards to the standards, discuss instead how to create integrated themes that span both grades.

In this way, you will have the opportunity to be free from your isolated silo, and see how learning connects to others outside of your four walls. This will take some focused work and initiative in the short term, but will create incredibly simplicity in the long run. By tailoring instruction around similar themes, you will be able to share resources, rubrics, and assessments. Instead of spending much of your preparatory time developing materials for class, you will be able to collaborate and learn from your peers.

Narrowing the focus

Once you have identified some common themes to plan around, consider which topics these themes might interact with. As stand alone themes, they are still too large. A science teacher can look at his/ her curriculum and work to revolve physics principals around the idea of balance, but not necessarily connect that same concept with the Maths teacher next door. A topical focus will allow for more organic integration, and ensure that your school doesn't remain a place for abstract concepts without real world application. Here are some topics you may consider that have and will remain crucial to understanding the developments of the 21st Century:

- Environment
- Economics
- Community
- Society
- Health
- Systems

By identifying these topics, naturally, ideas will be born for integrated, practical, hands-on projects. Projects provide these overarching themes a real world application and allow students to move to the abstract from the practical.

I'm going to get back on my soapbox. Forgive me.

How often do you hear teachers say, "Someday you will use this in the real world!" For much of my experience in high school with Calculus, this was my teacher's justification for asking us to solve for sin, cosign and tangents. World problems were impractical and relevant only if you happened to work in the 2% of fields that asked you to solve for such abstract values. "A hypothetical ladder leans against a suppositious wall in a conjectural way. The painter of the wall needs to know the measurements of the ladder's hypotenuse in order to lean the ladder against the wall without falling." The only thing real world about this problem was the fact that a painter may have needed to mount a ladder. However, how many painters do you know that use advanced algebraic formulas before they begin their work? When my dad painted walls in our house, he positioned the ladder according to a more valuable principle called "common sense."

Ok, I'm off my soapbox. Hopefully, you get my point. If we made math useful to solving everyday problems we encounter, perhaps students would see more relevance to learning it in school. Let's look at how to move from the practical to the abstract through an integrated project we recently completed in *Futures Academy* entitled "Project Blue Sky."

Project Blue Sky- A real world example

Anyone who lives in Beijing knows it suffers from bad air. In fact, as I type these very words, I'm staring outside of the bus into an abyss of gray skies. The AQI (a measurement of air quality) today is considered three times greater than the level deemed "hazardous." Ask any Beijing resident which problem they would seek to solve in the city, and I guarantee you nearly every response would be its air quality. And while the city has introduced measures to help counteract the high pollution in Beijing; with its growing population, increased standard of living and geographical location, it has been a failing campaign. A question that must surely be on the mind of everyone who lives here is, "How can we improve Beijing's air and water quality?"

This question is relevant, complex and certainly worth answering. It's an easily identifiable problem with complex math, science and Humanities principals lying beneath its surface. Without understanding these principles and how this content interacts and integrates, there is no way to permanently solve this problem. You see, the complexity of the integrated project arises from the simplicity of the initial statement.

This notion is counter- intuitive to the way in which schools have traditionally operated. The educational system has remained broken for several years because of the complex bureaucracy and systems managing its movement into the future. We talked earlier about human management systems and the need to delegate and divide oversight into small teams; the same applies to the management of content and paperwork. As teachers, we have become too bogged down in the minutia of content specific standards rather than the enormous potential of integrated themes. As a procurer of relevant learning, we've got to begin to think big picture. Here's a flow chart for how we arranged content within the integrated "Project Blue Sky."

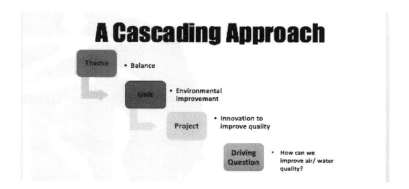

An ongoing debate in education is which should come first in the integrated planning process; the major theme or the subject specific standards? There are valid arguments on both sides of the coin. The educational purists insist the standards should come first while more progressive schools of thought argue that integrated project planning should start from a common theme. In my humble opinion, if I were a manager of the integrated planning process, I would tell my constituents that the starting point matters less than the eventual outcome.

What major understandings do you want students to reach? What allows you to align your curriculum's major goals into a simple statement? Personally, I have found that beginning with an agreed upon theme amongst all disciplines has allowed for the best integration. This theme is generally borne out of dissecting subject specific content, and seeing where there is overlap. Finding these big conceptual ideas allow for the most organic, real- world projects to arise.

So let's return to "Project Blue Sky" to show how the practical driving question of "How do we improve air and water quality in

Beijing?" allowed for the most abstract understandings to arise. As a team, we researched and thought about what people do in the real world to solve this problem. We looked at several innovations, interviewed creators of public policy, spoke with anthropologists who studied sociological trends to better understand how car companies can innovate moving forward, attended meetings held by NGOs working towards change, and finally, asked environmental engineers if they could advise the best route to pursue in helping solve this dilemma.

Typically, teachers in planning integrated projects go straight to their standards for learning. The only resource they have consulted is a static, complex document created by a team of educators who sat in a room and determined the most crucial material students should "know" and be "able to do." If we are to best serve our future tinkerers, creators and problem- solvers, we have to get out of this isolated way of thinking and expand our audience. I challenge you to get outside of your classroom as well. Before getting into the minutia of content specific standards, interview and meet with experts in the field you are attempting to explore. Chances are they will give you a better perspective on how to develop authentic projects considering they are the ones engrossed in exploration everyday.

This is not to say that standards are not important. Standards are crucial for vertical articulation as students move on through the program, to new grade levels, or to new schools. They provide the substance and depth for loftier, conceptual pursuits. But they are a means to serving a greater end goal, not an end in and of themselves. I will give you an example within the aforementioned project, *Project Blue Sky*.

A real world task we asked students to complete was writing an integrated proposal for how they would help improve air and water quality in Beijing. The proposal needed to provide an action plan for how to pursue their particular project in addition to a justification and rationale for the direction they decided to take. The document demanded an in-depth analysis of subject- specific content. Here are some of the *common core* standards the proposal had to include:

Science

- Construct a scientific explanation based on evidence for how the uneven distribution of Earth's groundwater sources is the result of past and current geoscience processes.

- Evaluate competing design solutions using a systematic process to determine how well they meet the criteria and constraints of the problem

- Identify consumers and producers in an ecosystem and the result of over consumption

- Identify and understand key components of the water cycle

Social Studies

- Develop compelling and supporting questions to guide an inquiry

- Determine helpful sources for answering compelling and important questions

- Explain the relationship between the physical and human characteristics of different places or regions

- Use evidence in a coherent argument to evaluate and

explain multiple causes for events

- Use the knowledge, skills, and understandings of Social Studies to take action on authentic problems

English/ Language Arts

- Integrate, evaluate, and analyze knowledge and ideas from a variety of informational texts and from multiple formats

- Write for the purpose of supporting a claim; employ techniques that correspond to these communication forms

- Research, evaluate and draw evidence from a selection of various sources to build and present knowledge

Math

- Analyze proportional relationships and use them to solve real-world and mathematical problems (calculating AQI and integrating within proposal)

It would be hard for anyone to argue that integrated projects lack a thorough investigation of content. Through a single final product in the context of a real- world project, students were responsible for thirteen subject specific content standards. And this is before students presented their material and began building! The opportunity to present this work to an expert panel afforded them even more opportunity to master English, Science, Math and Social Studies Standards.

How might you ensure this kind of integration occurs in the context of a project? You undergo the first three steps mentioned in the previous chapter. First, you create flexible schedules to immerse students in learning across multiple subject areas and disciplines; and second, you organize your space according to the type of thinking you want to promote. Finally, of utmost importance is that you carve out time to meet with the teachers you are coordinating with to build, reflect and ensure outcomes are reached.

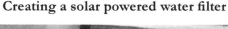

Creating a solar powered water filter

Integrated Rubrics

A problem we are going to inevitably face as procurers of futuristic, integrated learning is a lack of rubrics to evaluate student's mastery of these skills. Subject- specific rubrics are not enough to evaluate student's mastery in an integrated setting. Recall that we want to promote higher level thinking that is not confined by subject- specific criteria. Therefore, as a team, it is imperative you sit down with whoever you are working with and come up with the cross- disciplinary skills that you wish to collectively assess:

Skills like problem- solving if you have asked students to devise solutions to complex problems; or collaboration if the project asks students to work together on a team. Here are the cross-disciplinary skills that Futures Academy identified as being crucial to integrated work:

- Inquiry
- Critical Thinking
- Problem- Solving
- Communication
- Collaboration
- Innovation and Creativity
- Global Thinking
- Leadership
- Responsibility

Again, which skills you choose to assess depend entirely upon the scope of the project you develop. Let's take the example above regarding the writing of an environmental proposal. While we discussed how you might assess this piece in terms of subject-specific content, how might you assess it in terms of interdisciplinary skills? Clearly a well- written proposal demands standards of communication, but equally important is how well the proposal solves the underlying problem of air and water pollution.

How well-founded and thoughtful are the student's ideas and solutions? Are they grounded in research and relevant resources? Has the student tested out or prototyped the solution they are offering? Were they able to consider multiple perspectives? All of these questions constitute the way in which you format your "Problem Solving" rubric.

For re-usable rubrics already written around each of the above-integrated skills, please see www.bie.org.

A School Wide Approach to Integration

"We are only as strong as we are united, as weak as we are divided."- J.K. Rowling

Overwhelmed or inspired? Something tells me right now; you are feeling a mixture of both. You must be overwhelmed by the enormity of what I am asking you to do, but inspired by the implications it will have for your classroom and school. Remember, this is about making things more simple. If you take the time to re-structure and re-think your curriculum, you will free up, even more, time for you to do the things you love with students. Hopefully, as I suspect, you are the kind of person who has already envisioned how to make your classroom and school more integrated, while also taking the first action steps to ensure others are on board. This next section is intended to extend our understanding of integrated learning while also exemplifying the power a few like- minded individuals can have on the educational system.

A school- wide approach to Integration

If you teach in a PYP or MYP school, you have already been granted the freedom to integrate learning across common themes. The more conceptual MYP and PYP standards and thinking patterns have placed you in a prime position to integrate across subject areas with practical, hands-on projects. I was presented this opportunity when I taught in an MYP program for two years; between my time at High Tech High and the International School of Beijing. Etonhouse International School of Suzhou was a school that focused on "play- based, hands-on learning" and instructed students from age 5 to age 17. Class sizes were low with an overall student body of only 350. Problematic however was the fact that we still taught in isolated silos and came together only for weekly assemblies and major international events such as UN Day and the school's dramatic performances.

But our brilliant art and music teachers had a vision. Asked to instruct every grade level from early years to grade eleven, they needed a common curricular thread to stay afloat. They came together, dissected their subject- specific standards and decided that one theme was continually present. They were both required to look at the influence of past musical and artistic styles on today's work. They were both asked to teach students multiple genres in order to develop their individual styles. In other words, they were both asked to develop an understanding of their constituents of how the *wisdom* of the past helps us make better decisions in the present. The overall theme for a school- wide integrated unit was born: *Wisdom*. They had their theme, now all they needed was a practical way in which to deliver the major concepts.

Teachers across **all** grade levels were invited to come together to hear the art and music teacher's joint "visual and performing arts" presentation. Lounging back on couches and glancing at their watches, expectations of our staff was pretty low; this integrated unit was not only designed to deliver rigorous standards but also improve the culture amongst the staff. With confidence and eloquence, the art teacher revealed a multi-colored ribbon that would be the thread tying the whole school together. Practically speaking, it represented the multiple facets of "wisdom" that an old gypsy woman gained over the course of her life. Each strand embodied a different story or experience she had in her earlier years. In a dramatic production, she would sit a small child in her lap and reveal each story, one thread at a time. With 10 distinct colors, the ribbon spanned all of the grade levels present in our school. Each grade would be responsible for a different color and specific wisdom the gypsy woman would impart.

I was asked to work together with the grade 7 Math, Science, and English teachers to determine our theme. Being the pedagogically sound teachers we were, we immediately sought out our subject-specific content documents. We highlighted the content we covered earlier in the year in one color and the remaining content in another. On the whiteboard, we brainstormed the relevant ideas that seemed to cut across all subject- specific areas. After narrowing the themes down to a few that might work best in a joint performance, we came up with the theme of *sustainability*. More specifically, our story would originate in India, one of the oldest civilizations and originator of mathematical concepts, and revolve around the preservation of the modern day Ganges River.

In music class, grade seven students found songs that discussed the consequences of over-consumption. In art, students learned how to create watercolor paintings depicting the animals in India on the verge of extinction. In mathematics, students drew upon the "wisdom" of ancient Indian mathematicians to learn principles of geometry. In Social Studies, students analyzed the delicate balance between human production/ development and environmental sustainability. Finally, in English, students learned how to create narratives, develop appropriate characters and write scripts to map out the scenes that would tell this story.

Each week, the whole school met inside of the theatre to ensure continuity in the overall narrative of the play and integration across subjects and grade levels. After eight weeks, the whole school was ready to perform. Every single member of the school played a part. Some were permanent members of the band- the live soundtrack to transition from scene to scene. Some were members of the cast- acting out the narratives and stories written by their classmates. Some were directors- ensuring the smooth transition from class to class. Some were "stage hands-" moving props between major scenes to create the ideal setting.

The play was truly spectacular. But the most remarkable part of this story was not what happened before, or even during the production; it was what happened afterwards. When the curtains went down, the audience left, and the brilliant arts teachers received their plaques for their incredible leadership throughout the process, there was still work to do. A marketing team of high school students was responsible for selling and distributing the performance DVD along with a colorful insert to an interested market. These proceeds would help benefit local charities and pay for improvements in the theater for next year's production.

Questioning whether or not you can accomplish such a feat?

I definitely did. As idealistic and optimistic as I am for the power of integrated learning, even I had my doubts. But our school pulled it off; mainly because of the resilience of a few empowered individuals. Rather than get bogged down by the minutia of grade-specific benchmarks, fixed schedules, and bureaucratic oversight, they thought "big picture." They got the entire school engrossed in a vision and integrated learning around a simple, but profound theme.

You too have this power. You too can think big. And before

moving forward, let me be perfectly candid; it's also ok to think incredibly small. You can integrate learning with only one other subject, or even more realistically across two strands within your subject specific standards. The School-wide performances, integrated around common themes, are not something that a teacher new to integration creates overnight. Take small first steps. These steps *will* have an impact on student learning. They will represent the key first notches in your Integrated Professional Development "tool belt" to build confidence in your ability to integrate on a larger level.

An organization built around Common Goals: *Case Study*

The last example I provided demonstrated the strength of a whole school coming together for a common purpose. If you and a few other strong-willed teachers and administrators can achieve such integrated outcomes, you will have already been more successful than your predecessors. However, if we are to change the thinking of the entire system, as we have espoused to do from the onset of this narrative, we are going to have to get even more creative. To do that, I'm going to give you a practical perspective from one of the most innovative organizations in education:

Recall in the introduction how I mentioned *High Tech High*, the innovative school I left in San Diego. They formed an organization that began as a small coalition of schools that has now expanded to double-digit figures. How did they achieve this goal? They developed key design principles and common language for how they would integrate. After speaking with one of their founders, Rob Riordan, I learned that they centered their shared vision on six major principles.

§ **Personalization**: "Creating settings where teachers and students can know each other well."

§ **Adult World Immersion**: "Situating students directly in the world beyond school."

§ **Contexts for Reflection**: "Integrated, reflective contexts for students."

§ **Intellectual Mission**: "An articulated, common intellectual mission for all students."

§ **Community Partnership:** "Working closely with family and community."

§ **Teacher as Designer**: "Teacher as designer, inquirer, and clinician."

Establishing this shared vision created an appropriate context for the integration the coalition of schools would complete outside the classroom. In planning integrated experiences, one could always refer to the design principles to see if they fulfilled the overall vision. With enough small systems integrated around common principles, we can all shake up the system and provide a justification for getting outside our isolated worlds.

It's also important however to note as a precaution that integration is not an excuse for standardization. Unlike standardized tests, integrating learning around common design principles should allow for autonomy on how schools fulfill the vision. This is why Rob Riordan, when probed on how schools should integrate and interact insists, "We don't have a lot of structures for interaction between schools- we want them to be autonomous." [1]

In short, look for shared philosophies with which to integrate. These will provide a common framework for the experiences you create for kids and at the same time allow autonomy for how each school, institution or classroom fulfills this vision.

Team Teaching

Integration of subject specific content does not have to occur only in the context of overall unit goals; it can also live in the day-to-day delivery of lesson content. In my mind, there is no better way to deliver such learning than through a team teaching approach. But to build the impetus for such integration, I'm going to ask you a few key questions.

1. When is the last time you observed someone else teaching?

2. When is the last time you planned and delivered a lesson together with a colleague?

3. When is the last time you had an administrator in your classroom?

4. Where in the world does the growth of an organization occur in isolation?

If we are to hone, develop and refine our craft, we must venture outside our four walls.

After ten years of teaching, I thought I was pretty good at what I did. I had set routines, knew how to create a culture of risk taking and understood how to identify student strengths and differentiate according to need. It wasn't until my eleventh year, the one I currently find myself in today, that I realized I knew very little about teaching. That's because it wasn't until that pivotal eleventh year that I was able to observe daily lessons delivered by practitioners with techniques far superior to mine. I watched someone who planned transitions and lessons down to the very minute in which content would be delivered. I observed a master teacher who could pull twenty-three students outside, engage them in a rocket launch, and have them meditating face down on the floor ten minutes later.

Just imagine if I had never observed this artistry first hand; what a great disservice this would be for my kids. And so I'm asking you to do the same. Teaching is an artistry that can only be learned through careful observation of a master practitioner. Inevitably, the more you observe, the more you will build certain techniques into your repertoire. It will, in turn, reap huge rewards for student engagement and deeper learning within your own classroom.

In addition, after observing enough teachers, you will better be able to identify those teachers with whom you would like to deliver lessons together. Within our Futures Academy space, I have delivered lessons with both the Science Instructor as well as our Chinese Facilitator. Currently, we find ourselves in week two of a project that integrates all subjects around the simple but profound concept of "preparing for and responding to change." In Science, students study earthquakes and plate tectonics to better create and design their earthquake-safe structures. In Humanities, this understanding will lead to the lofty outcome of creating small social enterprises to benefit the local earthquake victims.

But how do these abstract concepts manifest themselves in a daily lesson?

In a joint "Humanities/Chinese" lesson, we looked at six major articles written around the recent quake in Yunnan, China to better understand the phases of earthquake relief, from preparation to the rebuilding. In a joint "Humanities/ Science" session, we then used this knowledge as a pretext for Science where they would learn important principles of tectonic plate movement in order to design and construct earthquake-safe structures. A secured partnership with a structural engineer has allowed students to be evaluated on real-world engineering criteria; the same real world codes that determine if homeowners gain approval for remodeling projects.

Through a "team teaching" concept, as a teacher, you will have greater control over the integrated process. You will be able to talk specifically about subject related content and how it relates to the big picture. This thinking will not come naturally for your students. You will need to constantly redirect them back to the simple concept that set the unit or project in motion. As a team teaching tandem, you will also have to dedicate yourselves to the planning process, ensuring that summative tasks necessitate the acquisition of all cross- curricular content.

An integrated team approach

Team teaching merely scratches the surface of integrated learning; if you want an even greater challenge, create a team that spans the entire grade level.

Every successful business partnership in the real world operates on this relevant premise. One partner acts as the visionary while the other acts as the voice of reason, balancing the organization's revenue, customer data and expenses. You too have your strengths. Are you the visionary who places few restrictions on possibilities, or the prudent and careful planner who wants to make sure everything is in the right place before moving forward? I've got great news; both are necessary. Who in your department or across your grade level helps compliment your personality and leadership style?

When ISB Futures Academy recruited, we sought to create this "perfect team." While I had clear strengths, my limitations were even more immediately recognizable. I was the "big picture" guy, who had no problem sharing a grand vision, but struggled with the more minute details. I could easily envision where schools needed to move in the future and could even draw a picture of what it looked like. At the same time however, identifying the 75 intermediary steps presented a great challenge. We needed someone with program development experience. However, unlike in traditional schools where you hire or outsource an administrator to oversee these functions, we instead elected for a teacher with this experience. This teacher would be actively involved in implementing our integrated model while also planning ways in which our program would expand.

One of my other weaknesses was in utilizing data to drive instruction and ensuing assessment. We knew in such a "high-stakes" model, we needed someone who was able to provide that data and make a compelling case for our new approach to learning. And similar to our "program developer/ teacher," this member of the team would be actively involved with our students.

I could talk specifically about every group member of our "perfect team," but that would not fulfill my #1 goal. My goal is to empower you, the reader to begin assembling your team. You may have waited in the past for an administrator to set the new direction for curriculum, learning, assessment, or program development. But remember, we don't live in that age anymore. Reach outside of your walls and begin forming that team yourself! Identifying your limitations doesn't demonstrate weakness, but on the contrary, emulates great strength. You have a network of collaborators only a few steps away.

Developing Assessment in an Integrated Model

Perhaps the best way to ensure integration within your classroom and school is by creating authentic assessments that allow students to demonstrate knowledge and skills across subject areas.

For example, in terms of our recent integrated unit on *preparing and responding* to change, as facilitators, we sat down before the project launch to determine what products exist in the "real world." Similarly, these products would serve as the summative tasks for our students as well. As teachers, we too often create assessments that simply do not exist in the real world. Assessments in the real world are a natural part of the project process. If you are building an earthquake-resistant home, a natural assessment of your progress is both the floor plan and inspection from the safety bureau. Our assessments must, therefore, include similar tenets. Likewise, if creating a business or social enterprise, business partners will have to write up contracts, create business plans and present those plans to potential investors. So too should our students in developing their social enterprises. Through tasks that challenge and engage students in integrated ways, students will come to acquire the minutia of more subject- specific standards.

Outside the four walls

"The education of circumstances is superior to that of tuition."- William Woodsworth

Now that you have integrated students with teachers and content outside the four walls of your classroom, you should be confident in integrating them outside the four walls of your school. You can be a beacon of light for your community, demonstrating the kind of innovation and risk- taking that will propel your community into the future. To visualize how you might integrate your students within a society and culture that exists outside of your four walls, I want you to complete an exercise that necessitates nothing more than internet connectivity, a pencil, paper, and an open mind.

You ready? Ok, here we go....

Go to Google Maps and type in the address of your school. Once the search engine has identified your location, zoom in to include all areas within 10 km of your school grounds. Next, screenshot the map or print directly from how it appears in Google Maps. Once you have the hard copy, grab a pen and circle every place that may represent a great learning experience for your students. Circle libraries, museums, parks, major design firms, organic farms and exhibition centers. Think outside of the box. Typically, when fulfilling academic pursuits, we value only places that are academic by nature; museums, libraries, and institutions of higher education. These are fine, necessary and beneficial to students; but many of them are still the isolated silos of research, disconnected from the rest of the community. Circle places that typically exist outside the realm of "schooling."

When you run out of ideas, turn to your curriculum documents. Circle places that represent key connections to the content you are responsible for delivering.

How might the world be your classroom?

In Futures Academy, we completed this exercise in the context of our units. We looked at our curriculum content, identified major themes, and mapped out authentic connections within the community. For "Project Blue Sky," we connected with the nearby wetlands and village; for the "Empathy Project" we joined with a neighboring Chinese School; and for our "Small Business" unit we linked with local non-profits and social enterprises.

Integration should never be an afterthought in effective planning. If it is, students will immediately identify the contrivance, and see the integration as a "field trip" rather that a natural part of their study. In other words, experiences can't be "one- offs." They should be crucial in students developing an understanding of the unit's goals, and more importantly, in developing their own understandings in the context of the integrated project. Let's return to our earlier example of improving air and water quality in Beijing for a more practical context for this concept:

In answering the question: "How do we improve Beijing's air and water quality?" we knew that students would need to look at current actions Beijing has already undertaken. Using these experiences as field studies allowed students to be more effective problem solvers themselves. Therefore, we identified a few of these solutions and looked at ones that were feasible in delivering in off- campus experiences. One was a trip to the wetlands to observe first hand the benefits of a natural ecosystem in water filtration. Another was a moderated interview with local villagers to find out how they receive and purify their water. The result of these experiences was a greater understanding of both the benefits and limitations of current approaches to water purification.

The picture below shows our students interviewing a local villager to learn more about water filtration:

Students interview local villager

If you teach at a more traditional school that has already identified field trips it will take throughout the year, make sure you alter them to make the trips more meaningful to students. For example, perhaps your grade level or specific subject makes an annual trip to the local museums to learn about history. The stretch of museums may include a museum on aeronautical engineering, one on prehistoric man, one on the evolution of dinosaurs, and one on horticulture and local plant species. Look at particular units you have developed or projects you have envisioned for the year and see which of these museums would be most conducive for a deeper study. When our Humanities class studied Archaeology and the progression of early man, a natural connection was to the Museum of Man. Students participated in a "mock dig" hosted by the museum curators, and in the process gained some important skills to successfully analyze the artifacts they would uncover later that week.

Building Justification for your Approach

A wise move for integration that will fulfill both academic and political gains is connecting to another prominent local school or university. Utilize your school's proximity to higher institutes of learning, and you will immediately gain support and perhaps even funding for your more lofty goals. At the International School of Beijing, facilitators did just that through the "Strategic Learning Office." This office was set up to forge connections with the community to deepen student learning while also providing a justification for the school's loftier strategic vision. In a week-long project driven week in the HS last year, several student groups utilized the most prominent University in Beijing to conduct their research. Tsinghua University agreed to act as a partner by providing lab space for students to conduct water and air quality tests. Their pricey equipment allowed for more thorough analysis while also providing students a glimpse of the kind of work they would complete when attending University later that Fall.

If University life is not in the near future for students, try partnering with a well established local school. In our unit on building *Empathy*, we consorted with the local Chinese school to complete home-stays according to student's interest and language levels. Like the integrated school, our community became one giant integrated classroom to pursue deeper learning goals. Lower level International Chinese speakers were paired with stronger Chinese English language speakers to ensure the richest development of language. As an additional benefit, students gained a stronger sense of the cultural traits of the community in which they resided. The result of the experience was a student panel coupled with first person monologues from the perspective of their partners.

Students with homestay partners

Some connections to the curriculum will not always be as clear. At the International School of Beijing, in order to better connect as a whole school with China, grade levels take part in annual "mentoring trips." While in the past, these trips have been impactful; they don't always leave a lasting impression, since one could gain a similar perspective by taking part in a tour by the local tour company. In order to make the trips more integrated with curriculum and to help students develop deeper understandings, the 8th grade Team used the mentoring trips in the context of their unit on advertising. In Social Studies, students explored the effects of propaganda on overall attitudes, while in Math, students studied how the most successful organizations used marketing to boost its overall revenue stream. The final product was an advertising campaign tailored to help the specific small businesses they studied.

Depth vs. Breadth

If you are to be engrossed in the meaningful work of integrating learning for your students, you must come to the realization that you may not give every standard in your curricular planning guides equal weight. On the contrary, and more importantly, you will develop the thinking processes necessary for students to make sense of new content they encounter.

For some of us, a statement like this is blasphemous to our sacred disciplines. Who am I to undermine the importance of students learning as much about ancient Egypt as they have been exposed to in ancient Rome? Or to imply that perhaps problem- solving is more important than knowing the variables of the Pythagoras theorem? Don't misunderstand me. Both pursuits are important. But too often, our vertical articulation of subject matter usually begins and ends in the minutia of subject specific content rather than the more lofty concepts and big ideas. Therefore, if your classroom or school is to move to a more integrated approach, you will first need to identify the thinking patterns and understandings that are most important to develop in your students. In my first school, the most helpful planning documents for integrated planning were subject- specific "Big Ideas." For Social Studies, these included the five most important topics for civilization development:

- Geography
- Economies

- Religion
- Government
- Technology

Which particular civilization students' examined was of less importance than understanding the impact the five topics above had on the civilization's development.

From our students

Again, as mentioned in previous sections, we must consider the most important question related to integrated learning: Has it impacted student learning? Here are a few of the quotes I captured from FA students in relation to that question:

"I think integrated work is the best and combines all of the subjects into a fluid motion so that when we switch classes we can basically just keep doing what we were doing in the previous class." - Alexis, grade 7

"One of the best things about futures is that all subjects in one or another are connected. I think that this is a good feature because it can reduce the amount of homework." - Cynthia, grade 7

"I think that one of the best features of Futures Academy this year is the integrated learning, it helps because when all the subjects have a direct correlation, you learn what you are learning faster." - David, grade 7

In Closing

Let's review our major learning about integrated learning before we move on to what is perhaps an even greater impetus for change in schools; individualization. First, recall that integration best occurs within the context of your existing realities. Before approaching an administrator and demanding that shared common planning time, you must demonstrate that integration is valuable and impactful on student learning. Start by reevaluating an existing unit and look for cross- curricular connections. Reach out to that teacher next door. Chances are you both share a homeroom or common section. Use this shared class to deliver an integrated lesson. If you start small, you are less likely to talk yourself out of delivering the kind of learning that we all know is most powerful for students.

Our other important learning relates to the power of team teaching. This idea is even easier to implement, as all of your colleagues will have at least one prep/ flexible period throughout the day with which to coordinate. Team teaching will have two major impacts on your practice: First, it will impact your students. Students will benefit from having more individualized attention, as there are two adults to deliver learning. Second, it will impact you as an educator. You will witness first hand a style of delivery that differs from your own and learn some valuable lessons on how to improve your practice. As a teaching team, you will have the opportunity to reflect on the integration and improve for next time.

Finally, integration has the power to impact the whole school if building around common themes. Start from the 1,000 foot view before getting microscopic with learning. What major understandings can you rally discipline specific learning around? Sustainability? Entrepreneurship? These "big ticket" items have several implications for subject- specific standards. This type of integrated learning will make learning relevant and meaningful for your students. Now that you have dipped your toes into the world of integrated learning, it is time to immerse yourself in making education more individualized for your students.

[1] *Rob Riordan*, E-mail correspondence from January 13, 2014.

CHAPTER FOUR

INDIVIDUALIZED OPPORTUNITIES

"Everybody is different. Everybody deserves to be given an individual plan that's best suited for them." – Johnny Almarez

W
hat do you like to do after a long day of work? Are you a sports nut who can't wait to turn on the tv and check the latest sports scores? Are you a father or mother of a young child and can't wait to play hide and seek with them before the sun goes down? Perhaps you are a sci- fi junkie who can't wait for the next issue of Popular Science. Personally, I love to play music. When I sit in front of my piano, it's like my whole world shuts off. I feel free and totally in tune with what I'm doing. Music is my language; it boosts my creativity and brings me complete joy. I could sit in front of my piano and play music all day long if it wasn't for that nagging responsibility of work.

Many of our students operate the same way. That seemingly unmotivated student that hangs in the back of our classrooms and struggles to complete even the simplest task is the same student that can sit at the free throw line for hours perfecting his shot. On the basketball court, there's no need for a watch, he'll never check it.

What if we structured schooling in a way that allowed all students to shine? What if instead of asking our students to fit the narrow confines of our curriculum, we asked our curriculum to fit the wide range of our student's interests?

In the past, this was an impossible task. Our limited technology and inflexible textbooks only allowed for one way of learning. Bobby, our star athlete, either excelled or floundered. There was little room for delivering curriculum according to his interests. Fortunately, we don't live in that age anymore.

Online Curriculum

We no longer live in an age where teachers, in order to be effective, have to generate the curriculum themselves. Software developers have done the hard work for us. Online programs can crunch numbers and chart paths for our students; progressing them at the appropriate pace while offering feedback and insight into the learning gaps we need to fill. As mentioned in previous chapters, we can shift from our roles of the "deliverers of content" to the "facilitators of learning." In this way, the high fliers can advance while the struggling students like Bobby can receive the extra help they need.

In Futures Academy, we have used online curriculum to help individualize learning for our students. Similar to your students, our students all came at the beginning of the year all with varying levels of proficiency. Differences were most stark in Math. Some students entered 7th grade not knowing how to add and subtract integers while others came ready to factor polynomials. In a traditional program, with only one method of delivery, these students would be forced to learn at the same pace, and cover the same content. And while the struggling students would certainly benefit, the high fliers would be held back. With an online program however, all students can grow at a rate appropriate for them.

Let me introduce you to the best friend we made this year; his name is derived from his ingenious creator with the help of a fairly wealthy software engineer. Meet "Khan Academy." This online curriculum assesses students current proficiency in varying math concepts; spends five minutes creating an individualized curriculum; and then shoots out "problem #1." If students answer the first question correctly, they are advanced to a slightly more difficult problem, and if incorrect, there is an explanation (generally a youtube video) dictating where they most likely went wrong. Students can earn badges as they advance through levels and even collaborate if they would like to work from two separate places.

And while it is pre-emptive to claim complete success, Khan Academy is clearly proving to be successful. On the MAP test- a measure of "academic progress" used by many International Schools to evaluate programmatic success, whereas an average school experiences on average 50% of students achieving growth goals, 90% of Futures Academy students met or exceeded their growth marks last year. Some students grew by as many as three proficiency levels.

At present, there are two students who already completed the 8th grade math curriculum with only two months left in their 7th grade year.

Think of the implications a program like Khan Academy can have for you as a teacher. Rather than spend hours generating math problems, differentiating them for your students, checking for understanding, and finding time to meet with students who missed the concept, you can simply monitor their progress online. In addition, with your flexible space and newly formed table configurations, you can group students according to their proficiency levels and deliver small lessons to each group.

If you don't have enough time to get to each small group, you can empower the small committees I spoke about in the first section. Form a small committee of math "peer tutors" who can act as your support facilitators. Ask your math whiz who completed the 8th grade curriculum to help little Alice with her fractions.

Again, let's return to that sticky question of, "What is your role as teacher?" Hopefully, the answer to that question is becoming clearer. Through an individualized approach, your role is simply to work with students in setting goals, monitoring progress on achieving those goals, and supporting them if falling behind. You are the coach who helps guide and support your students to learn themselves.

Conquering your standards

Beyond individualizing learning for your students, online curriculums will also help ensure you cover standards so that you can spend time fostering deeper learning opportunities for your students. As a Humanities Teacher, online curriculum has been invaluable in covering the minutia of the language usage standards. Our students use a program called "IXL" which is specifically tailored to the grade 7 standards, allowing them to select a specific skill and then advance through the sub- set of questions. Similar to Khan Academy, problems increase in difficulty and students earn badges upon completion of each skill.

I want to be clear that I am not advocating for online curriculum to replace you as the teacher. You are still the brilliant mastermind behind ensuring the mastery of content. I'm only making a case for online curriculum as a way help you work more simply and efficiently.

Empowering other students

If hoping to successfully institute online learning in your classroom, make sure to distribute oversight responsibilities. It would be unfair to assume that a single adult in the classroom could ensure individualized programs for all students in class. Some of you see over hundred students on a daily basis, each with varying levels of needs. Therefore, if we are going to successfully facilitate individualized learning, we are going to have to empower others to act in our place. In Futures Academy, we have instituted a peer tutor program to fulfill this aim. To become a peer tutor, students must reach a designated level of proficiency at which point they are given a bracelet and a team of students to coach. It is not uncommon during math lessons to find four students huddled around a peer tutor as they work out algebraic computations on the table. Multiply this by six, and you have your class covered. Meanwhile, you can provide one on one conferencing to those students with profound misunderstandings.

Empowering the individual

We spoke earlier about online programs helping map out student's learning path in the mastery of content; but what if students charted out their learning paths for deeper learning? What if you provided them with the entire curricular body of what you had to teach, and asked them to learn on their own?

Would they be successful?

Some would. These are the same students who ask for a rubric before you finish explaining the instructions; or for early

95

submission before you have even notified them of a deadline. These are your high fliers. They are the same students who would make even the novice teacher feel like a veteran.

If you are lucky, you get maybe two of these students in each of your classes. The rest of your students are going to wait for you to tell them exactly what to do, how to do it, how long they have to finish, and what they should start on first. This is how schooling has been for them for as long as they can remember.

But there is a problem with this kind of delivery. First, students are not encouraged to make meaning of content and learning on their own; and second, it's not sustainable. Students will become dysfunctional the minute you step foot outside of your door.

What if things looked different? What if every kid in your class was motivated and self- directed? What if they were so in tune with their learning styles, passions, and dispositions that they could be self- directed regardless of the task? Think how much easier your job would be. This kind of individualization can happen, and I'm going to tell you exactly how to do it.

Goal Setting

If you are going to be successful with individualized learning for students, you are going to have to start by teaching students how to set goals. For many students, this will be a very difficult task. They have grown so accustomed to basing their goals on a teacher's expectations, that they will not know where to start. They will think of goals in broad categories, making statements that they want to "become a better reader," or "get better grades." This is usually where the goal setting process ends for them, not understanding the importance of establishing check marks to ensure progress. Imagine saying that you are going to retire by age thirty without having a roadmap to guide you there. By age 29, you will be frustrated that you have not even saved a penny. Likewise, without realistic goals and a clear road map to get them there, students will not know how to chart their learning paths.

What's the starting point for goals?

Asking students to simply set a goal is not enough; we need to provide them with feedback tools to make those goals most relevant to their areas of need. One of the greatest feedback tools we used within Futures Academy was diagnostic testing at the beginning of the year. Students participated in the aforementioned MAP test, which assesses students' skills in math, reading and language conventions. Once finished, the test identifies the band of which the student most likely falls; indicating what skills they already have, in addition to skills they most likely need to gain.

For example, a student's results might show that they test quite high in literary analysis but very low in the comprehension of informational texts. This information is crucial in providing direction for what kind of reading you engross students in, and the reading skills you explicitly teach to improve their comprehension. Similarly, in developing language, you might note that students are capable of organizing their writing, but lack the fluency skills to make their writing engaging for a reader. You can then extract and promulgate these skills through small, focused writing sessions with other students who require similar supports.

But you or a test that identifies areas of need will not be enough. And unless you want to spend countless hours analyzing, compiling and collating data, you are going to need a more efficient system in getting individualized results for students. My suggestion is to put this analysis in the student's hands. After handing back student scores, and subsets of data, explain how students can analyze that data to set goals for growth. Imagine the impetus for this kind of self- evaluation. Instead of Johnny indicating that he wants to "improve as a reader," he is now able to articulate that he wants to improve in "identifying how the author uses indirect characterization to develop characters." Not only does Johnny sound scholarly, but he also has a focused area for growth that can lead to the appropriate novel choice.

Finding the Time

Where do you find the time in your already packed schedule to offer individualized learning opportunities for students? The answer to this question lies in instituting some of the philosophies of the last section. Now that you have created integrated blocks of time to plan around, you can also look like a team that offers individualized learning time together. Find a period of time where you and another subject teacher overlap and then share a space together. Once you place the students in the shared space, ask students to work on the online curriculum most appropriate to their needs. In this way, students will receive the extra support they need in each subject while also having you as an additional resource to answer any additional questions they may have.

Sink or Swim

Because of our busy schedules and plethora of content to cover, most of us have a "sink" or "swim" approach to delivering the content. Students either get it, or they don't. Regardless of their level of proficiency, at some point, we as teachers just have to move on. We know this isn't sound pedagogy, but because of scheduling, we just simply don't have the time to re- teach concepts.

What if you were able to free up time in the schedule to offer struggling students additional help, while at the same time ensuring the high- fliers are able to move on?

Empowered with your new integrated approach to learning, you can make this happen. Work with another teacher to offer a shared time for "catch up."

In *Futures Academy*, we have utilized blocks called *Learning Lab* to ensure students have mastered concepts. We begin the block by asking students to identify where they need help, and then find the appropriate teacher to assist. Similarly, teachers also have the opportunity to identify the students they need to see. We keep track of the offerings in a shared timetable, viewable by all students. This is referenced below:

Subject	Offering	Time	Room	Students
Humanities	Short Story Review IXL work	1st half of block Ongoing	Small table in back half of room	Individual conferences- will call to table
Math	Algebra- Extra practice w/ Mrs. W Unit 3 Test Results	1:20-1:40 1:40-2:00	Conference Table Conference Table	Christopher, Timothy Luke, Karina
Chinese	Conferencing about video work	When not with other teachers		Mark, Jimmy, Bobby, Kristine

An Individualized Reporting System

Pictured Above: Individualized portfolios for students to exhibit work.

We call it "The Hub" but our kids call it the "Nexus." Personally, I like their choice better. It's the only way to describe it. It's an informational reporting system straight from the future; allowing kids to compile and post work to demonstrate their learning, analyze relative areas of strength; and keep up to date and organized with assignments in all subjects.

Remember that road map for goal setting we spoke about earlier? That's what this reporting system represents. It was the prototype of two years of research. Our school spent two years identifying the most important skills we wanted students to gain and then put together a reporting system that provided guidance to students on how to get there. Imagine as a parent, opening a webpage that featured a multicolored wheel, with each color representing one of the following unique headings:

- Creativity and Innovation
- Communication and Collaboration
- Inquiry, Critical Thinking and Problem- Solving
- Leadership and Responsibility
- Global Thinking

Now imagine clicking on one of those colors and finding a portfolio of work from your student designed to demonstrate proficiency in that particular skill. The portfolio is filled with videos, presentations, PDFs and pictures created and edited by the students themselves. Would this be a good indication of how your child has progressed as an individual?

Imagine if you are the student responsible for posting work. You notice that while the "Creativity and Innovation" portion of your wheel is nearly full, the "Leadership and Responsibility" section is severely lacking. After clicking on this portion of the wheel, you find vivid descriptions of what kind of sub-skills are necessary to demonstrate proficiency in this category. Might that direct you in setting specific goals?

This system has also helped students in documenting their growth in relation to each of their goals. By the end of each unit of study, it is expected that students have a portfolio filled with work samples of their achievement.

Reader's and Writer's Workshop

If you teach Humanities, you are in a prime position to deliver individualized, passion- based learning for all of your students. Thanks to the worldwide web and sites like "Pinterest," we have several diagnostic tools, mini-lessons, and resources to begin using with students that are only a click away. Within ISB Futures Academy Humanities, one of the most powerful ways we have individualized learning is through reader's and writer's workshops. These mini-workshops provide students with the tools to analyze literature or create written compositions according to their passions or the integrated unit of study. I care less that Johnny is able to complete a worksheet on parallel structure than I do transfer the skill to a piece of writing he is passionate about.

Workshops begin with a targeted strategy for the day, followed by teacher modeling of the strategy within their chosen book or piece of writing, individualized time for students to practice transferring the strategy in their own work, and finally, a pair/ share discussion to solidify the learning for the day. As the facilitator, you can circulate during independent work time and offer specific support as to how students develop each successive skill.

Colombia University has some fabulous first-hand research and seminars regarding the power of reader's and writer's workshops on student achievement. I can tell you first hand that I have seen my student's writing ability grow tremendously! Some students, once timid writers, have now written entire short stories; others have transformed from struggling readers into avid readers once given tools for how to make sense of their reading.

Letting Go

An essential tenet of individualized learning is the willingness to let go. The most effective managers are able to delegate the plethora of responsibilities to their constituents, in turn creating a series of small systems that manage themselves. So too must you put students in charge of their own learning if hoping to be successful. We spoke about the relevant systems you must enact to create individualized learning, now we will talk about how to develop those relevant skills.

Leadership and Responsibility

If students are to take charge and lead their learning, they must first learn skills that all effective leaders possess. Engage your students in small leadership tasks. Sit students in a circle, and ask one student to lead the group in organizing students in an alphabetical line according to last name. Give them one minute. Next, pick a new leader, draw a series of shapes on the board and ask them without talking to assemble in the same formation. Incrementally increase the difficulty of the task, and ask new students to take charge. Reflect on the experience and identify obstacles that prevented them from completing the task promptly. Similar to these activities, explain that students must also identify the obstacles that will prevent them from charting their self-directed learning paths. Time, miscommunication and task confusion will be the same obstacles students face when trying to achieve their individualized learning goals.

You, as a facilitator of individualized learning, can find opportunities to engage students in activities that develop the skills you are trying to hone, without being overly prescriptive. By doing this, you will develop the buy- in for what you are trying to

103

achieve.

Here is a statement from our students that captures how Futures Academy has developed them as a self- directed learner:

"One of the best features of Futures Academy is the freedom. This freedom that FA has provided students has made students much more mature and responsible. I've seen some of my peers go from being immature students to students that are mature and focused that take responsibility for their actions."- Michele, grade 7

That's a pretty bold statement from a 7th grader. You too will see your students develop this ability of reflection when giving them more individualized opportunities.

In Closing

As a seasoned practitioner, individualized learning demands you work smarter, not harder. By letting online curriculum do the hard work for you, you will have more time to focus on supporting students according to their individual needs. Individualized learning will also allow you to empower your students to chart their own learning paths. Setting clear boundaries and structures for goal setting will ensure that they take responsibility for their learning and check- in with you when falling short. Finally, by working with students to create portfolios of work, you can ensure they document their learning process while being able to reflect specifically on their growth throughout the learning.

Now that you are empowered by developing self- directed learners, it's time to learn how to develop a community of innovators.

CHAPTER FIVE

CREATING A COMMUNITY

"Culture eats strategy for breakfast"- Peter Drucker

U pon completion of the first semester of my teaching credential, I thought I knew it all. I knew about differentiation, lesson planning, scaffolding, assessment, and even how to engage the unmotivated student. I knew what to do when technology wasn't working and how to organize groups according to learning types. I was like many other twenty- two year olds, who knew way too much about strategy, and way too little about culture. Imagine my chagrin when stepping foot into a 10th grade classroom that fateful first day to a room full of teenagers whose only concern was, "Am I going to like this guy?" Rather than engage them in a story of who I was, why I was there, and what I hoped we would all gain from our shared experience, I immediately jumped into the "anticipatory set" for the lesson; the driver for the objective I hoped to achieve. Needless to say, they were uninterested. Sure, they obliged, and the class never erupted into chaos, but it set the tone for what would be a very tough semester of student teaching.

"Culture eats strategy for breakfast."

Creating a positive classroom culture starts with developing a positive learning community. If the 21st Century is about student ownership of learning, as facilitators, we must find out exactly what makes each of our student's unique. Unlike in the past, where it was about getting students to respect you so they could be open to what you had to share, today's narrative is about getting to know each of your students so you can learn from each other. What are their likes and dislikes? What kind of instruction works best for them? Are they auditory, visual or kinesthetic learners? How do they take to feedback and criticism? Are they sensitive and in need of constant praise? Or are they thick skinned and in need of clear expectations? Are they the creative type who benefit from multiple ways to complete assignments? Or might they need direction to maximize their potential?

Discovering answers to these questions will help you establish a positive classroom community that fosters risk-taking and innovation. Below are strategies guaranteed to create this kind of culture.

Circle Time

Remember in kindergarten where the whole class sat around a rug and listened to stories about mythical heroes? While I am sure you do not remember the details of the story, I am certain that you remember the feelings of the shared experience: Your teacher perched atop a wooden chair; a storybook as large as her body opened wide; your classmates cross-legged on the floor next to you. Story time was a collective experience that the whole class could enjoy.

Perhaps you never had story time in kindergarten. Perhaps the time your class gathered in a circle was at the beginning of the day where Mrs. Smith would discuss the learning for the day before leading the class in an interactive activity.

The activity you completed is of less importance than the relationships the activity promoted. Students and teacher were equals. It was as if you were all learning together.

There was not the traditional hierarchy that exists in most classrooms. Fast forward to middle and high school where learning becomes more segregated, with rows of chairs facing a board or projector at the front of the room. While this kind of learning is necessary at times, it has been given an inequitable share of instructional time.

Have you taken the same approach with your students? How do you begin each day with your class? Or if you are an administrator, how do you encourage your staff to begin each day? How do you guarantee equity? The culture you create on the first day of the year, and likewise, in the first minutes of each class, will set the tone for the relationships you develop for the rest of the year.

Becoming a facilitator of learning

In my early days of teaching, one of the first things veteran teachers insisted I create was a classroom discipline plan. "Without solid classroom management, you won't even be able to teach." This, they insisted would establish the hierarchy, and me as the authority in the classroom. And while I agree a classroom management plan was important, especially in establishing my authority in the class, the plan was only as good as the relationships I developed with my students. Despite setting clear expectations the first few days of the year, I found my first few years of teaching to most tumultuous because I valued the demands of my content over the needs of my students. I was the "sage on stage" and students needed to respect that.

This kind of student to teacher relationship will not fly in the 21st Century. Students can receive the same content we hope to deliver in a far more engaging and intelligent five- minute youtube video. Establishing a positive classroom culture in your classroom is the #1 method to ensure effective classroom management. Therefore, if we are hoping to be relevant in a fast moving, ever- changing age, the relationships we establish must be much more egalitarian than they were in the past. The diagram below illustrates this point:

Similar to class "circle time," by positioning yourself on an equal level with your students, you will have the most dramatic effect on student learning. This will naturally shift the delivery of instruction to be more discussion oriented, rather than lecture based. Learning becomes a conversation that allows everyone to contribute. I will give you an example of how to position yourself as a facilitator of learning through the delivery of a Social Studies lesson.

Start by transforming a standard deck of cards into a medieval social hierarchy. Articulate each role in the hierarchy by writing a description on the back of each card. Face cards represent royalty and as such get the most comfortable seats; they must speak in old English, and only interact with other face cards. If approached by a lower card, these people must bow and kneel before uttering a word. Lowest cards can only speak when given permission and can never under any circumstance speak directly to face cards. Assign various roles to other cards so that each class has a clear position and understands how they must interact with others in the circle. Explain that during the proceeding simulation you will merely act as a moderator.

Finally, sit students in a circle and explain that "today they will be transported to the past to experience life from a new perspective." Distribute the cards and ask students to assume their role. As the facilitator, provide topics of discussion centered on student interest, and moderate the proceeding conversation. Ask questions that probe and challenge student thinking. Create make-believe scenarios that cause disruptions to the existing hierarchy, placing peasants atop the social class ladder, and royalty at the bottom. Look for "teachable moments" throughout the activity by which to deliver the content.

This kind of discussion will serve two purposes: First, it will allow you to discuss the hierarchy that existed in medieval Europe while also alluding to the kind of hierarchy (if any) that should exist in the classroom. Bring out a huge flip chart and ask students to brainstorm expectations and agreements for the relationships that should exist in class. Narrow the list down to five that everyone in the class can agree upon. This will help establish the positive culture your classroom needs to thrive.

Socratic Method

As mentioned previously in the section on *Individualized Learning*, students must direct their learning to be successful in the 21st Century. To start this process, you must first teach students how to ask the right questions. Direct them by modeling how to ask good questions, and how to seek out and discover the answers. In this way, students will learn how to utilize you to guide them in the right direction and re-focus them when they go off course. This "Socratic" and "Constructivist" approach to learning allows you to form distinct relationships with each of your students to better meet their individualized needs.

This Socratic relationship serves the most practical purpose in the context of an inquiry-driven project. In ISB Futures Academy, as facilitators, we used this approach in all four units of study. The student- driven inquiries allowed us to teach the appropriate discipline specific content without being overly prescriptive. For example, in the unit on "Change Driving Innovation" we asked students to generate relevant inquiries around the needs of earthquake victims. Next, we asked them to seek out the answers. Through mini- lessons, field trips, expert testimonials, and hands-on experiences, students were better able to understand human needs, and in turn, develop appropriate social enterprises to help meet them. They also felt empowered to direct their own learning.

To be successful, the Socratic method demands that you first engage students around the outcome you hope to achieve. Pose authentic real world problems that need to be solved and ask students to discover solutions themselves.

Think of yourself as a coach rather than a teacher. As a coach, your job is to develop your students so they can flourish on their own. The learning each day represents the practice your students will go through in preparation for the big game. Finally, think of the "big game" as the final performance task your students will complete to demonstrate their learning.

One on One and Small Group "Coaching"

Many of you teach in classrooms with high teacher-to-pupil ratios. In my early days of teaching, I taught at a school with a 30:1 ratio. My responsibilities included teaching five classes a day with three separate sets of curriculum spread across three different grade levels. Practically speaking, my major goal for those years was to "keep my head above water." Some of you face a similar if not more daunting dilemma of having way too many students, and unrealistic expectations of how you are supposed to meet their individual needs. I can only empathize and offer my continual support. However, regardless of the circumstances from which we come, we can all do a better job of developing individual relationships with each of our students. I have found one-on-one and small group coaching to be two of the most practical ways to achieve this.

To develop better relationships with students, you have to decrease the time in which you deliver whole class instruction, and increase the time you deliver individual or small group facilitation. Here's what a typical lesson should look like:

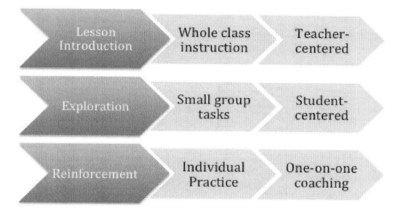

Note how the bulk of the lesson allows for the teacher/ facilitator to meet with individual students. While this time can certainly be relevant to the lesson just delivered, it also can be related to the student's overall needs: It can simply be a "check-in" with the student in regards to their overall feelings towards class and progress towards their goals. Would I expect that you reach all students in one day? Certainly not. That would be both unrealistic and unproductive. However, if you spread the one-on-one coaching over the course of a week, I am confident you could hit all of your students.

In ISB Futures Academy, we oftentimes met for one-on- one coaching during "flexible" blocks of time. These blocks of time saw students working towards individual goals with their facilitators available to offer additional support. As students worked independently, we called students one at a time to meet with us for consultation. These times were crucial in developing relationships with our students. Some students needed suggestions for online tutorials including vocabulary and language development while others needed specific time and project management strategies. Whatever the needs of the student; they became far easier to address in a one-on-one environment.

Recognizing student achievement

Simply put, students are not recognized enough for their achievements. While we pay close attention to academic achievements, oftentimes it is the same students receiving these awards. These include the infamous "student of the month" awards, "dean's list," and "honor's" recipients. I am not arguing to get rid of these awards as they certainly motivate some students to achieve new heights, however, for a majority of students, they only widen the gap between what they are capable of and what they actually achieve. When we recognize students for a wide range of categories and skills, we help foster the relationships crucial to student success.

Within ISB Futures Academy we recognize students on both a daily and weekly basis. Daily, during our morning mentoring

112

sessions, after our initial greeting, we give students the opportunity to recognize their classmates for various achievements. Students always begin with, "I would like to recognize _____ for." We have only two rules for recognitions. Students must be kind and specific. Here are some examples of the kind of recognitions students offer their peers:

"I would like to recognize Bobby for helping me learn how to factor polynomials."

"I would like to recognize Lauren for being a great group member and completing her work on time."

By honoring each other publicly, students re-enforce their personal relationship while also fostering a positive classroom culture.

Bracelets

As mentioned previously, an academic award does not motivate all students. Even less are motivated by the traditional paper awards given at awards assemblies. Where do these paper awards end up in the long run? I have several, stuffed in a drawer deep within the bowels of old boxes that sit inside my parent's attic. In order to be effective with recognizing student achievement and not ostracize them from their peers, we have to offer awards that kids actually think are "cool." You may or may not have noticed that several of your students wear bracelets to support various causes. I have seen students wear "boobies" bracelets to support breast cancer awareness and "blood donor" bracelets to acknowledge their commitment to disease eradication. Beyond acknowledging their altruistic commitments, these bracelets simply look cool. ISB Futures Academy from the beginning of the year jumped on the bracelet bandwagon by creating several of its own to honor the various achievements students made throughout the course of the program. We identified the 10 most important 21st Century Skills, consulted with students on catchy bracelet designs, and then ordered the bracelets in bulk from a local supplier. During circle time each week, we honor students for the specific achievements they made that week to exemplify each skill. To ensure equity, the facilitators maintain a spreadsheet to keep track of bracelet winners and the skills they were recognized for. The bracelets have greatly encouraged student engagement, but most importantly, they have motivated students to pursue skills that are most meaningful to them.

Peer to Peer Relationships

As a facilitator of learning in the 21st Century, you possess the unique ability to not only ensure an equitable teacher-to-student relationship, but also an impartial student-to-student relationship. With students who come from all different backgrounds, ethnicities, families, personal preferences, and experiences it is imperative that you develop strategies and activities that expose students to all of their classmates. By exposing students to classmates who possess great similarities and also marked differences, you will ensure a positive classroom culture for student achievement. Here are some strategies to develop these relationships.

Personality and Learning Style Activities

At the beginning of the year, ISB Futures Academy knew that if it were going to put students in control of their learning, it would have to institute activities that allowed students to better get to know themselves and their classmates. When prompted, each student would need to know exactly how he or she best learned, interacted, participated, and problem solved. To achieve this

114

amount of self- knowledge, we created various groupings early in the year based on specific test inventories. One test built around student preference gave students a few scenarios and asked them to choose which situation they most preferred. At the end of the test, the algorithm aggregated scores and presented students with a colored wheel to indicate their preferred learning styles. The learning styles were based on Howard Gardner's work in multiple intelligences:

Ø **Kinesthetic**: Hands-on learner. Great physical coordination.

Ø **Visual- Spatial**: Learns best through visuals. Can manipulate shapes. Can identify individual parts and how they fit in the whole.

Ø **Auditory**: Great with oral instructions. Impeccable memory. Can recount specific parts of a story.

Ø **Interpersonal:** Learns best by working and interacting with others. Very sociable. Likes to talk through things when solving problems.

Ø **Intrapersonal:** Great self- awareness. Introspective. Very independent. Works best alone.

Ø **Musical:** Recognizes musical patterns. Talented.

Ø **Naturalistic:** Can sort and categorize. Learns best when surrounded by natural environment.

Next, we placed students in homogenous groups and asked them to represent their learning styles on a large sheet of poster paper. Understandably, the way they interacted with each other and presented their learning style was in direct parallel to the way they best learned. The kinesthetic learners worked together standing up, with one student juggling a ball and another fiddling with his pencil. Their poster included lots of balls, bats, hockey sticks and sporting equipment. The visual- spatial learners immediately gravitated to the stack of rulers and fine point pens, intent on getting the shapes on their poster exactly right. They drafted, erased, edited, and re-drafted before the poster met their final approval. The auditory learners struggled with their poster. Because they were so accustomed to learning through oral input, they had a hard time representing this input on the paper. The interpersonal learners always undergo a similar struggle. Since they are so interested in pleasing each other and making sure everyone's voice is heard, they tussle on coming to agreement on what the poster should look like. They would much rather interact with each other with no set outcome then have a deadline they had to fulfill. The musical learners laid the paper out on the ground and took spots on each corner. With headphones lodged firmly in each ear, they drew guitars, musical notes, drums, sticks and some logos of their favorite bands. There was no set organizational structure for their poster as they were content with letting each member do their own thing. Finally, the naturalistic learners, after taking seats on the back couch, calmly decorated their poster, showing great patience in the process. They spoke to each other in soft, calm voices.

This activity in and of itself spoke volumes to the kinds of relationships that would exist amongst classmates. Some students would work best in a calm, relaxing atmosphere while others would need music and constant movement to thrive. When each group presented, as a facilitator, I made reference to the needs of

116

each participant in the class. I posed probing questions that forced students to see beyond their preferences to meet their classmates' needs.

How might you help your students recognize the needs of their peers? If you are an administrator or school leader, then what kind of workshops or PD might you develop to ensure colleagues get along?

I find the beginning of the year to be the best time in which to complete all of these personal inventory tests. It ensures that you establish the kind of culture guaranteed to foster success amongst your constituents. A practical next step you might take once you have completed the inventories with your constituents is to create colored note cards for heterogeneous groupings throughout the year. Create stacks for the following categories:

Ø Learning styles

Ø Leadership styles

Ø Personality types

Ø Favorite subjects

Once you have created the stacks and color-coded them to indicate differences, pair or group the cards together heterogeneously according to the assignment you are asking your students (or colleagues) to complete. In this way, your constituents will be exposed to several ways of learning, interacting and getting things done.

Pair/ Share

Another way to ensure successful peer-to-peer relationships is through giving students a chance to converse in a relaxed setting. Arrange the classroom with 12 sets of chairs, each facing each other. Next, give your students letters, either "A" or "B." Have the "A's" sit down first. Finally, ask the "B's" to take a seat across from one of the "A's." Place a prompt up on the board or projector and determine which student will be the speaker, and which will be the listener. Give students about two minutes to converse and then ask the "B's" to stand up and find a new partner.

Mentoring/ Homeroom

We've talked a lot about the importance of establishing a positive culture in your classroom. This ensures healthy, constructive relationships amongst all your constituents. Now it's time to discuss how to nurture those relationships. Too often, we leave the social-emotional development of our constituents to irregular times at both the beginning and end of the year. I'm going to discuss how we can make this part of our daily schedule.

"A beginning is the time for taking the most delicate care that the balances are correct." –Frank Herbert, *Dune*

The start of each day is the most precious 30 minutes you will have with students. This crucial window of time sets the tone for learning and ensures balanced, positive relationships throughout the day. Again, the best format for this start is by forming a circle with your students. I suggest mixing up the seating to ensure students have the opportunity to sit beside a new classmate each day. In our classroom, we achieve this by placing name cards on random seats when students first enter. You might also number students off and ask them to sit next to their partner. Once students are seated, we move into a daily greeting. Greetings could be as simple as finding students with the same color shoelaces and telling them "good morning." They can also be complex, asking students to greet the students born farthest from their birthday month. In my mind, the greeting is the most important part of morning mentoring. It is a way of saying, "hey, we recognize you and are glad you are here." No matter what kind of morning students had, they know that they will be acknowledged simply for being present at school. After morning greeting, we like to give students an opportunity to discuss a topic relevant to either the current unit of study, a community event, or their personal lives. By creating a safe space for this discussion, you acknowledge that your students also have a voice. Rather than lead this discussion as a whole group, ask students to discuss the topic with an "elbow partner," or someone close by. This helps guarantee that more introverted students have a space to share. Once students have completed discussing the topic with a partner, open the conversation up to the group. To ensure equity, spin a marker to randomly give four people the opportunity to share. After about 5 to 10 minutes of sharing, move into an interactive activity that gets students up and moving around. We like to play games like "zip zap" and "murder winks." These quick, interactive games are highly engaging and help stimulate the brain for the learning that will take place for the rest of the day. You can find many of the descriptions for these games online. Finally, we like to end mentoring for each morning with the daily announcements. This is the time to inform students of major events happening within the school. In our school, these events are updated daily and can be found on the school's website. I have seen other schools that include these announcements as part of a daily bulletin by student council that transmits over loudspeaker or via a tv monitor. By allocating time for these announcements, you help reinforce that your classroom is part of a larger community.

In ISB Futures Academy, we take 25 minutes for morning mentoring. For many of our students, it is their favorite part of the day. When given a survey about what to increase and decrease in ISB Futures Academy, a high percentage of them responded by asking for more morning meeting time. It is here where they feel connected and that they are a part of something. It is a chance to warm up their brains and be acknowledged.

Relationship with the Community

If we are going to harness the kind of relationships most relevant to the 21st Century, we have to become comfortable with receiving critical feedback. Think about the way in which you determine whether or not a business, school or organization is successful. Even with the most carefully crafted mission statement, school banners, or self- endorsement, your assessment of the school is probably going to be based on two critical criteria; data and ratings. Like most, I am confident you will utilize tools like Yelp, parent feedback, and specific data for how the school measures up against others. Data from test scores will provide a window into the level of academic rigor the school provides while ratings will give a more important glimpse into the kind of culture the school fosters.

In the absence of community ratings and a personal "Yelp" for your classroom, you are going to need some kind of feedback measurement tool to ensure the most positive interactions with students. In ISB Futures Academy, we designed and administered surveys at the mid-way point and at the end of each unit of study as a barometer for how well we were achieving major goals. After reviewing the surveys, we looked for emerging themes to discuss in face-to- face discussions and interactions with students. We divided a white board into two halves; one for "things we are doing well" and one for "things we need to improve." We added an additional column later in the discussion for "solutions." We appointed one student to act as the student facilitator to help lead the discussion and intervened when things got off topic.

This process is not easy.

Making yourself vulnerable to criticism takes a lot of humility. Students (and parents) might offer criticism that strikes a nerve. However, by taking this crucial step, you are sending a message to your constituents that you value their input and opinions.

You will build trust amongst your students and in turn transform the culture of the classroom and school to one that values feedback.

Another way to elicit daily feedback is by making a visible spot for "suggestions." Give it a creative name like, "making class (or school) awesome" and follow up on them regularly. I suggest every few days. Address the suggestions as a class and determine ways into integrating the suggestions into your daily routine. This will add to a culture of openness and ensure you are addressing everyone's needs.

Building relationships amongst staff

Earlier we discussed the importance of integrating subject specific content to ensure the richest learning experience for our students. Some might assume that simply by insisting a focus on integration will ensure collaboration and positive relationships amongst staff; and while this will certainly encourage various constituents previously placed on opposite ends of the school to increase face to face time with their colleagues, without clear structures in place, learning will take the same form it had in the past. For the integration to be successful, you as a change agent must ensure that these structures are in place.

Group Huddle

How do you begin each morning? Chances are you find yourself in your office, staring at a computer screen desperate to finalize that last slide or print off those copies of supplemental handouts before students arrive for the first period. Or perhaps it's with a watered-down Americano in the teacher's lounge with some colleagues. For many of us, the first conversation we have will be with students in mentoring or in our first period class. I would challenge us to change this routine. We spoke earlier about sharing office space with colleagues to facilitate greater collaboration, and imposed some structures to ensure this happens, and I would like to suggest another. It's called the team "huddle." Much like summer camp counselors would get together before starting a long day with campers; we too should get together before facing a long day with our kids. The team stands in a huddle with the facilitator starting the discussion. The facilitator begins by asking everyone to greet and then discusses some important reminders for the day including:

Ø Major announcements

Ø Schedule

Ø Upcoming events

After the facilitator speaks for three minutes, each team member has one minute to either respond or pose a question related to something that may have been missed. The huddle follows a strict protocol, allowing team members to discuss only those items that can be **quickly resolved.** In this way, the team huddle serves two purposes. First, it allows coverage of redundant meeting agenda times, and second it helps nurture and support healthy relationships amongst staff. Despite the fact that after the huddle, teachers may still teach in their isolated silos, at least, they feel connected to other team members.

We always end each huddle by placing our hands in the middle, and raising them together with a chant; much like a sports team does before a major competition. Sounds cheesy right? But trust me, this is completely intentional. We want students to experience the energy we feel. If they see their teachers collaborating and teaming in such a way, it will also trickle down into the relationships they share with each other.

Critical Friends

When I began my teaching experience internationally, both in Suzhou and Beijing, I was immediately paired with a colleague who served as point person for understanding the intricacies of the school and its functioning. If I had questions regarding curriculum, school policies, tech systems, etc., they were my initial line of defense. They were my "critical friends." Having these peers proved to be invaluable in understanding the status quo, but I felt that the relationship was oftentimes too one-sided. It often involved me coming to them in high-stakes situations, in need of quick solutions. I often lamented that I could not help them as much as they could help me. In the 21st Century, we need a relational narrative that is more equitable, allowing for two- way communication that pushes both participant's thinking. I suggest critical friends both within subject-specific departments and grade level teams, and outside of your assigned teaching role. In this way, you can receive continual feedback on your classroom practice while also ensuring successful alignment of shared values within the entire school. Here are the structures that will allow these critical friends to be most meaningful in fostering 21st Century relevance:

Goal Setting

After establishing critical partnerships, your first task should be to develop goals that align with shared school- wide values. By aligning your goals to these shared values, you establish the most important tenets of a positive relationship while also providing for a critical feedback tool. Any change you institute can and should be aligned to these underlying values. It also allows your critical friend to provide constructive criticism when activities or strategies you implement don't noticeably align.

Common Meeting Times

Once you have set your goals, decide on a time to observe each other. This could be in a class you teach, a meeting you facilitate, or any other opportunity you have to lead a group. Following the meeting or class, sit down with your critical friend and ask for feedback. Your friend will start by reminding you of your shared values and pose key questions that allow you to reflect and develop.

Keep track of your meetings in a spreadsheet. Document the contents of the lesson or meeting and the self and peer evaluation of how things went. Over the course of the year, these documents will comprise the foundations for a reflective yearly evaluation of how well you achieved your goals.

Staff Digital Portfolios

In the same ways we ask students to continually develop their repertoire as learners; we too must develop our repertoire as leaders. We must consistently immerse ourselves in professional development which should include self- and peer evaluations, forums for discussion, and educational research. But most importantly, we cannot hoard the learning all for ourselves. We must also seek to disseminate our learning to others. In this way, we can strengthen our overall practice aligned to our shared values.

A practical approach to this goal is through the development of digital staff portfolios. These digital reservoirs should embody the bulk of work you are completing to develop as an educator. They should include resources, activities, reflections, pictures, and videos that leave no doubt in the mind of your colleagues of how specifically you have strengthened your practice. Just imagine a collection of staff portfolios that span all subject areas, grade levels and positions in the school. These important artifacts will strengthen relationships as they will signal a commitment to learning and growing together.

In Closing

Establishing a positive learning community will allow your students to engage in the kind of risk-taking and innovation necessary to transform your school. Your newly created structures for developing this community including homeroom, Socratic discussions, and group recognitions will help honor this community and allow for its development. As a facilitator and leader of this newly formed group of innovators, you will be able to model growth by the way in which you interact with others in your school.

CHAPTER SIX

REAL WORLD EXPERIENCES

"We cannot solve our problems with the same thinking we used when we created them."- Albert Einstein

When are we ever going to use this?

I have a confession. It's quite an embarrassing one given my focus in university and chosen career path as a Humanities Teacher. Please refrain from making quick judgments. Here it goes. I used to hate history class. I know, crazy right? As a kid, I saw it as nothing more than a useless assembly of facts that had no relevance to present challenges. My history teacher saw things differently. In addition to identifying key events and important world leaders, he demanded his students copy down exhaustive timelines in their notebooks that spanned the given period of time. I used to complain at home to my unsympathetic parents and do impressions of my aging history teacher over an evening meal.

But one fateful day, as a teenager, I built up enough courage to question the relevance of learning history. I remember our teacher rambling on about a civil war battle and the generals who led each side when I raised my hand to question the relevance:

"Mr. Brewer. When will we ever use this information in our real lives?"

Mr. Brewer did not seem caught off guard. Already woefully unaware of how the class perceived him, he had a quick response that could satisfy only a teacher of history.

"We learn history because if we don't learn about the past, we are doomed to repeat it."

I heard this quote uttered before. I vaguely remember my dad using it in reference to a political campaign and saw it plastered to the bumper of an old car. I'm sure it stated something of great importance. But to a thirteen- year old kid who was mostly worried about joining the right sports team and doing his best to fit in, it was meaningless. I did not foresee becoming a military general any time soon or warring against my relatives from neighboring states.

In 2015, many classrooms and schools still operate according to the same faulty premise. We assume that information we perceive to be useful will also be perceived as useful by our students. In math class, we still ask students to solve problems in which they purchase 35 cantaloupes and 25 watermelons knowing full well they will never encounter such a dilemma in their real lives. We demand that students write essays and timelines on political topics they will never confront. We require kids to create 3d models of the inside of the earth because we did the same thing when we were their age. Oftentimes, instead of tailoring our instruction according to what students "need to know," we tailor it to what is "nice to know." We inundate students with principles inherent to the world of school rather than those easily found in the real world.

Today's classrooms and schools demand a new narrative. Like the real world, our classrooms and schools need to encourage students to see the bigger picture. We cannot isolate learning as a series of unrelated concepts and facts. The real world is integrated, highly complex, and unlike traditional curriculum, very hard to define.

So how do we accomplish this goal? We re-structure the existing curriculum:

Practical to Abstract

Let me make one thing abundantly clear; I am not in favor of re-**writing** the curriculum. A collection of brilliant educators, leading thinkers and brainpower far superior to mine spent several years developing the curriculum that exists in schools today. You will be hard pressed to find a person who deems reading and writing as obsolete in today's integrated society. Similarly, understanding and utilizing the scientific method will help in any pursuit, regardless of whether or not you are a scientist. My simple point is that we as educators need to **restructure** the curricular content to better align with real world pursuits if we hope to serve our students. Here's an example:

Improving air and water quality

I mentioned earlier that I reside in Beijing, China. It doesn't take a scientist to observe that much of this city's water has been polluted. A foul smell emitting from any spring or river, coupled with discoloration and the need for chemical treatment tells you that the water source you are observing is not safe to drink. Similarly, when you observe gray smoke released from a factory stack, you will probably rightfully observe that it is causing air pollution. However, what's more important than the observation

129

is the very practical conclusion that something needs to be done about it. The problem is that without extensive knowledge of how particular filtration processes can be improved, or an understanding of the actual production processes existing within the manufacturing plant, there is not much you can contribute. This illustrates the concept of how **practical** observations and pursuits can lead to **abstract** thinking.

This is generally how the real world operates. Complex organizations with several interdependencies, expertise, and abstract ways of thinking generally align themselves around a simple, practical outcome.

So too should your school align their curriculum.

Imagine this; instead of curriculum being aligned according to the following structure:

1. **Subject**

a. *Subject Related Idea*

    i. Content Standard #1

        1. Benchmark #1

        2. Benchmark #2

        3. Benchmark #3

2. **Subject**

a. *Subject Related Idea*

    i. Content Standard #1

        1. Benchmark #1

        2. Benchmark #2

        3. Benchmark #3

We aligned according to this structure:

1. Concept

a. Cross- curricular content

      i. Benchmark

      ii. Benchmark

      iii. Benchmark

b. Cross- curricular content

      i. Benchmark

      ii. Benchmark

      iii. Benchmark

c. Cross-curricular content

      i. Benchmark

      ii. Benchmark

      iii. **Benchmark**

Think about how easy it would be to integrate curriculum across subject- areas with this new approach. Understanding the minutia of the subject-specific content would be secondary to understanding how to utilize the content in order to grasp the main concept. In other words, standards would serve as a means to a greater end. Students, through being able to see, touch and feel the content you hope them to grasp will be more likely to engage in the abstract principles your curriculum demands they acquire.

Building Connections to the World Outside of School

Who are the collaborators in developing the units and curriculum for your school? Chances are they are mainly educators who

131

reside in your building. Or perhaps they are located off- campus in a District Office or administrative building that oversees several schools. Perhaps you do not have collaborators at all. You may have the unfortunate task of developing the entire curriculum in isolation within the confines of your classroom. While schools have sought to build stronger ties within a network of educators, they need to push beyond the world of school and connect with organizations in the real world. Schools need to connect with NGO's, tech companies, small businesses, architecture firms and hospitals. Here's how:

Attend Networking Events

Teachers and administrators need to be allotted time to attend networking events within the community. While these networking events are generally tailored towards high- powered business executives or leaders of industry, they will also serve our most high functioning schools. Imagine the admiration you will receive if informing others of the event that you are "an educator seeking to learn more about the real world." I have used this line in nearly all the networking events I attended. It is generally received with a chuckle but later develops into an enlightening conversation that provides me insight into how the real working world operates.

I bring this knowledge back to my students for one purpose: To make their academic pursuits more relevant. I have attended NGO networking events hosted by local pubs, start- up fairs organized by local entrepreneurs, and future city planning meetings arranged by local architects. They have all been gracious in allowing me to ask questions and observe.

Where's the starting point?

I suggest starting with an integrated unit of inquiry and then brainstorming the possible connections to the outside world. When devising the unit on social entrepreneurship, I knew that I needed to learn a lot more about small- business creation if I was going to impart the knowledge to my young students. I started by reaching out to an entrepreneur from our school board. He helped start four businesses and coached young entrepreneurs on how to make their start- ups successful. After a few meetings, we determined that it would be most beneficial if he coached our students in the development of their small business ideas centered on disaster relief. He taught our students how to create and deliver an elevator pitch, assemble their prototypes, and how to determine projected costs. He even sat on the panel to judge the viability of our students' enterprises.

Think of how useful this connection was to our team of facilitators in the long run. Structuring our project successfully meant collaborating with someone from the real world on how they structure their start up projects. Our entrepreneurship project also involved an expert from the scientific world. Since we asked student's small businesses to focus on disaster relief, it seemed fitting that they learned a bit more regarding structural engineering. And similar to the approach we used with our expert entrepreneur, we sought out a structural engineer to learn of the process they undergo with young engineers. As a result, she helped deliver the opening activity to our unit, which asked students to create the tallest free- standing structure using basic household items. When students finished building, she used their simple structures as a window into the complex world of structural engineering.

These examples provide the most adequate narrative for the shifting role of the teacher in the 21st Century. In the 20th Century, as teachers, we would have felt obligated to learn every concept of entrepreneurship and structural engineering before imparting the knowledge to our students. Next, once we finished this learning, we would then assemble a series of slides to impart this knowledge to our students. We would teach them about structural engineering without ever asking students to pick up a hammer, or create their business plans.

Connecting students to the real world in the 21st Century demands that educators work "smarter" not "harder." They must develop and utilize the vast networks around them if they are to make learning truly meaningful for their students.

Passion Projects

Many of us belabor the vastness of the curriculum we must cover in a given school year. We barely have time to cover key concepts within our own subject- specific disciplines, let alone make relevant connections to the outside world. But I'm going to let you in on a little secret, by re-structuring your curriculum to be more relevant to your students, not only will you be able to cover the concepts dictated by your subject- specific standards, you will make learning more exciting for your kids. A successful company took this same approach.

Most of us would consider Google a successful company. In addition to amassing massive amounts of capital and profits, they have changed the way in which the world operates, thinks and communicates. Most of us would also assume that to achieve such breakthroughs, their employees must work into the deep hours of the night and have monumental expectations on the projects they are asked to complete. But this assumption is wrong. It operates on the premise that equates great work with long hours. But that's not Google's secret. In Google, great work is a direct result of employee enjoyment and engagement. They believe, and rightly so, that work will be most productive when employees have a stake in the final outcome. To allow ample time for these individualized pursuits, Google has created a concept called "20time." This time is allocated time for employees to work on projects they are most passionate about. It also happens to be the time that has produced some of the company's greatest breakthroughs. Ie. The hot air balloon that delivers wifi to rural villages; or the self- driving car. As an employee in this tech conglomerate, you are guaranteed that 20% of your time will be filled with personal projects you are most passionate about. The only stipulation: It must somehow benefit the company.

Let's take this same approach to schooling. Imagine the productivity and engagement we can foster within our students if offering them 20% time.

In ISB Futures Academy, we have designated these blocks of time as "passion blocks." For two blocks a week, students can pursue anything they are passionate about as long as it carries some benefit to society. Here are some of the projects our students chose:

- Novel creation
- Building a robot
- Creating "eco- friendly" bags
- Rooftop gardens
- Documentary filmmaking

In developing their projects, students were forced to establish a budget, create a timeline for deliverables, connect to a mentor, and blog regularly about the work they completed. Similar to the way Google and the "real world" operates; most projects arose out of a simple passion and resulted in the establishment of an innovative breakthrough.

Passion Project- creating reusable bags

I can probably guess what some of you are thinking right now. "Sure, passion projects are great for a school that supports this kind of self- driven pursuits, but I have way too many standards to cover." I'm not going to begin to fault you for thinking in this way. Of course, it is nice to have an administration that supports this kind of innovation. Some of you teach in incredibly demanding systems. But again, rather than abandon or defy the burden of content you are responsible for delivering, why not work with it? Build this stipulation into student's individual pursuits. Lay out every standard you are responsible for covering over the year to the students, and ask them to think of creative ways to connect their passion to the content. You will be surprised what students think up.

Presenting to experts

Once you have formed the invaluable connections to the "real world" existing outside of school, look for ways in which students can present their work to experts in the field. Invite those initial collaborators that you met with earlier to act as judges for student work. Imagine the value students would receive if having their engineering projects judged and assessed by actual engineers. Think of the impact that would have on their learning.

As a facilitator, you have the opportunity to create these experiences for your students. You do not need to start too big. Find a competition in the local area that will allow your students to get out into the real world and interact with experts. I'm willing to bet that if you did a little research, not only could you find competition, but more importantly, you could find an authentic connection to your content. And as is the case with any good networking, once you find a few contacts, they will lead you to several more.

In Futures Academy, we utilized our network outside of school to set up many experiences for our kids. One of our best connections to content was a competition called "Futures City" in which students had to design a no waste city. Our students competed against students from throughout China and presented their work to real engineers and city planners. The picture below shows our students on competition day (they took 3rd place overall):

Students presenting to experts

Partnerships/ Internships

We discussed this concept earlier, but I want to revisit it in relation to students' more individualized pursuits. Remember when we had courses like shop class? Or home economics? These courses operated on the assumption that learning should be just as much "hands" as it is "head." Where are these classes today? Many have been removed from the curriculum as there is just "not enough time" to allow for these pursuits. This unfortunate reality has placed America far behind the rest of the world in its number of scientists and engineers.

In this rapidly advancing innovative age, we need to foster the development of as many skills as possible in our students.

However, I propose a new narrative for the integration of these kinds of courses in today's age. Rather than mandate students take "home economics," "engineering," or "small engines," instead, build courses around student's passions. Naturally, you will have some students who are adept at using their hands to build, while others will know how to program in computer languages that have not yet entered the college curriculum. Find out what students are interested in, and then build real-world partnerships around those interests.

In ISB Futures Academy, we took this approach and found some great success. When learning that some of our students were interested in our small arduino circuit boards, we partnered them with a robotics programmer to help them build their first robot. When we discovered that some students had interest in horticulture, we partnered them with our facilities manager to explore the possibility of rooftop gardens.

The partnerships were organic. I'm willing to bet that if you polled every member of your school for what additional skills they have beyond teaching, you would find a staff with an eclectic mix of talents to offer your constituents. In addition, I am sure your parents also have an eclectic mix of expertise to offer. Before beginning each project or major unit of study, inform your parents of the learning objectives, and then inquire of parents what services they might be able to offer. If the project involves the construction of artificial buildings or city planning, reach out to parents you know are engineers. If it involves idea creation, reach out to parents you know that are entrepreneurs. In this way, students will immediately see the value of their academic pursuits, and in turn, increase the quality of their work.

Internship- Creating a bamboo bicycle

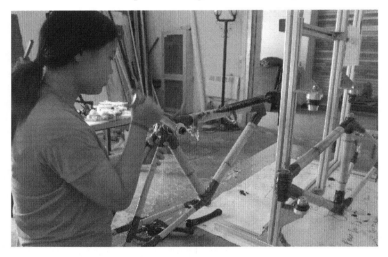

Innovation Academy: *A Case Study*

There's a large international school in the heart of Lima, Peru that makes internships a mandated part of the program. To keep in step with a rapidly changing 21st Century, the school decided it was too big to offer this kind of sweeping changes to all of its students; so instead, similar to *Futures Academy,* they decided to form a small wing of the school called *Innovation Academy.*

This academy's mission is to help students find their purpose by "creating a culture of intrinsic learning and ongoing innovation." (3) In my mind, that intrinsic learning and ongoing innovation are best exemplified by their internship program. Students pick an area of passion, ranging from marketing to investment banking, and spend 60-80 hours every week shadowing and working with real experts in the field. Some are even paid for their service!

How did they start this program? By reaching out to those most invested in their students; their parents. Imagine the delight of your parents when articulating to them that you hope your students can get 'hands on' experience at their own firms. Some of the companies the Academy works with in Peru include: Belcorp, The Diner's Club, BPZ Energy and a marketing firm called "Mambo." These burgeoning corporations are large players in the international global market, and they were all accessed through an authentic connection.

Remember I started this book and told you to start from envisioning what kind of change you had control over? It's no secret that the most successful schools implement this very ethos. By reaching out to your parents, you too can form real world experiences that would be impossible to orchestrate had you contacted the companies directly.

Start with the End in Mind

As is the case with any good planning, it helps to start your planning with the end in mind. Think of products students can create that will serve value in the real world. Perhaps you are studying the environmental issues in the region and conducting a field study on the local water sources. What will students create that will add value to this topic? Have them team up with local biologists to create a field guide for the average consumer. The more you engross students in real-world tasks, the better equipped they will become in creating real solutions.

A Solid Floor with an Unlimited Ceiling

Real world learning creates a solid foundation for students while also allowing for an unlimited ceiling for what they might produce. The world of education, by contrast, creates an uncertain foundation, clouded by complex, unrelated curriculum documents and matrices of standards and expectations. I urge you to create that solid foundation for your students. Allow the complexity to arise in the exploration of real world tasks. Start students off with something they understand and encourage them to ask the right questions to discover answers they do not know. In this way, your students will be motivated to produce work of exceptional quality.

IN CLOSING

We live in an exciting time for education. The 21st Century has revolutionized our field. The internet has transformed the way in which the world communicates while software programs and advances in communication have allowed us to work smarter and more efficiently. Yet we are underutilizing these key resources. It's time to change that. While our schools historically have lagged behind these developments, it's time for them to now be the frontrunners. We serve the most adaptable creatures on earth- our children. We have an active work force comprised of billions of students ready to contribute today. But we've got to provide them with the right tools...

Flexible scheduling will allow schools to adapt, integrate and individualize learning for their students. Students will be given the opportunity to see how learning connects. They will also have the chance to set personal goals and organize their time to best fulfill them. In a similar way, schools will structure their time more efficiently to help meet the needs of all their learners. The new paradigm will be the reconfiguration of learning around those our schools they intend to serve, rather than asking students to adapt their way of thinking around the institution they attend.

Flexible space will provide the atmosphere to promote the kind of thinking and problem-solving patterns we want our students to develop. Movable walls will allow teachers to break down the barriers between content to allow students to make connections. Writable surfaces will make thinking visible and foster the kind of collaboration that leads to solutions. Easy to maneuver furniture will allow for multiple groupings and configurations, giving students the opportunity to be part of several interdependent teams.

Integrated learning will allow schools to work more fluidly around common goals. Just as the workplace is integrated around project related tasks, so too will schools. When parents ask their children what they learned in school, students will no longer have to rattle off a series of unrelated concepts and facts, but instead be able to articulate the bigger picture. Teachers through teaming structures will be encouraged to collaborate with each other to simplify their curriculum and goals.

Individualized learning will allow schools to meet the needs of all learners. Schools will no longer utilize one common method of delivery with outliers being given "special support," but instead treat all students as individualized learners. Through helping students identify areas of challenge and setting goals to help overcome them, students will be empowered to take control of their learning. In turn, when these students become our future citizens, employees, and degree holders, they will know exactly how to contribute.

Healthy relationships between staff members and students will provide the support structure to allow for the most radical changes in the 21st Century. Through collegial coaching, a strong mentoring program, and shared leadership, staff and students alike will feel empowered to reach common goals together. A culture of constant reflection, feedback and growth will allow schools to take greater risks and reach new heights.

Finally, by providing real-world contexts for learning, schools will help connect students to the world outside of school, and give new meaning to their academic pursuits. In this way, students will find learning to be a simpler, more fluid process that is clearly connected to the outside world. Students will be empowered to create products of real value, tied not only to a learning objective but additionally, to a real world issue.

We are breeding a culture of action. You read this book because you identified yourself as a change-maker. You are a doer; a pioneer who is too ambitious to wait for the whole route to be mapped out before taking the first step. While I have presented you with many scattered pieces of the puzzle, it is up to you to start making sense of it. Commit today to changing, at least, one way in which you do things. I promise that regardless of the outcome, it will empower you to have the confidence to change many more. Finally, thank you for being part of the greatest profession on earth.

Works Cited

1. "The Dalton School." *Dalton School ~ Mission Statement*. Dalton School, n.d. Web. 06 Dec. 2014. http://www.dalton.org/philosophy

2. "Company – Google." *Company – Google*. Google, n.d. Web. 04 Dec. 2014. http://www.google.com/about/company/

3. Topf, Corey. "Innovationacademy." *Innovationacademy*. Creative Events, n.d. Web. 22 Jan. 2016. http://www.rooseveltinnovationacademy.com/#!ia-culture-new/ce2k.

ABOUT THE AUTHOR

Kyle Wagner is the founder and lead consultant for "Transform Educational Consulting," a consulting group that empowers school leaders to improve instructional practice and student learning through innovative programs and teaming structures. He is also the former coordinator of Futures Academy at the International School of Beijing; a program that uses interdisciplinary project- based learning to connect students to their passions and the world outside of school. Kyle is also a former educator at High Tech High and holds a M.Ed. in Teacher Leadership. When not writing or teaching, he is performing with his original band, singing karaoke at KTV's and traveling the world with his partner. He currently resides in San Diego, California where he spends time developing schools of the future and helping other school leaders build theirs.

E-mail him at kylewagner@transformschool.com or visit his website at www.transformschool.com to schedule a free consultation.

Made in the USA
Columbia, SC
24 March 2022